SPIRIT SEEK

Words from Scriptures That Transform Your Life

LaTonya Branham

BabyStar Productions

Dayton, Ohio

SPIRIT SEEK: WORDS FROM SCRIPTURES THAT TRANSFORM YOUR LIFE

Compiled and Designed by LaTonya Branham

Published by BabyStar Productions
P.O. Box 1271
Dayton, OH 45401-1271
www.LaTonyaBranham.com

Library of Congress Control Number: 2007907484

ISBN-10: 0-9787296-1-7
ISBN-13: 978-0-9787296-1-5

Cover: Marion Designs
Printed in the United States of America

~To both of my grandmothers ~

Ruth McCorry and Inez Allen

Internally beautiful, praying women

~~~~~~

Favour is deceitful, and beauty is vain: but a woman that feareth the Lord, she shall be praised.

Proverbs 31:30 (KJV)

~~~~~~

Contents

Foreword
Introduction 1
The Old Testament 2
The New Testament 4
Agape 6
Abundance 8
Believe 10
Bless 12
Compassion 14
Direction 16
Endurance 18
Everlasting 20
Excellent 22
Faith 24
Fellowship 26
Forgiveness 28
Free 30
Friend 32
Fruitful 34
Gift 36
Giving 38
Grace 40
Grow 42
Heart 44
Holiness 46
Holy Spirit 48
Honor 50
Hope 52
Humble 54
Inspiration 56
Integrity 58
Joy 60
Knowledge 62
Leaders 64
Life 66
Light 68
Live 70

Lord 72
Love 74
Marriage 76
Mercy 78
Obedience 80
Peace 82
Power 84
Praise 86
Pray 88
Priorities 90
Promise 92
Prosperity 94
Repentance 96
Righteousness 98
Salvation 100
Seek 102
Soul 104
Spirit 106
Strength 108
Success 110
Teach 112
Thankful 114
Transformation 116
Truth 118
Understanding 120
Victory 122
Wisdom 124
Worship 126
Zeal 128
Knowing God 130
Child of God 132
The Twelve Disciples 134
Women in the Bible 136
The Beatitudes 138
My Spiritual Companion 140
Acknowledgements 141
About the Author

FOREWORD

Challenging, Devotional, Inspirational, Instructional and Provocative best describe LaTonya Branham's latest work, *Spirit Seek*. Suddenly, meditation on God's Word has reached a new plateau as this inspired author invites her readers to contemplate the scriptures through a collection of devotional narratives supplemented by challenging word find puzzles.

An emerging star among literary artist, LaTonya Branham intrigued us with her first project, *CultureSeek*, a cutting edge approach to the study of African American History. *CultureSeek* has now become a natural segue from the historic past of African Americans to discovery and nurture of our spiritualities through this creative study of the Bible.

Spirit Seek comes to us at a time when so many are bereft of hope and disillusioned about the future. All too often, the description of human interaction around the world is weighted with one episode after another of chaos and crisis. Throughout the world, the aisles of popular bookstores are filled with people in search of a written word to equip them with resources necessary to meet huge personal challenges we all face in life. *Spirit Seek* offers a new reservoir of devotional reading that merges our thirst for divine inspiration with our appetites for leisure activity and intellectual stimulation. This book provides spiritual guidance for every season in life. Whether celebrating a significant achievement or facing a formidable life challenge, *Spirit Seek* is an aid, engaging the Word of God in the transformation to a better you. Keep this text close to you. You will find it helpful during quiet time throughout the day. Carry it with you to school or work. Make *Spirit Seek* a traveling companion as you move about the globe. Rely on this book as a companion to your personal Bible Study. *Spirit Seek* is an excellent resource for pastors and Christian educators in search of relevant curriculum materials for their new disciples orientations and special Bible Study groups. Families will develop and grow from *Spirit Seek*, as they gather in the home for meditation and study. As *Spirit Seek* readers unlock the door to a myriad of stimulating word find puzzles, it is likely they will also discover the key to resolution of numerous personal challenges as well.

Postmodernism has rarely witnessed the measure of selflessness demonstrated by Branham as she liberally shares with the world her God inspired giftedness, thus ushering her readers into the presence of something far greater than themselves. With graciousness, humility and a whole lot of style, Branham reaches into antiquity to bring the voice of God face-to-face with a new generation who fully appreciate the need to pour new wine into new wineskins.

Dr. Thomas D. Johnson, Sr.
Senior Pastor
Canaan Baptist Church of Christ
Harlem, New York

Introduction to Spirit Seek

~~~~~~~~~~~~~~~~~~~~~~~~~

"Let the words of my mouth and the meditation of my heart be acceptable…" What is considered acceptable depends on what you feed your heart and spirit and how the message is received. If your thoughts are negative, then your words and actions are likely to be the same. What are your favorite words? Do they positively feed your soul and spirit?

Spirit Seek was uniquely designed to help reinforce and manifest the words inspired by God in your life. It is obvious to many that the world is in need of a positive transformation in order to develop better relationships within the family, community, workplace, government, schools, places of worship – and most importantly – with God. Every opportunity you have to positively develop spiritual character is a great way for you to draw closer to God. Words form Scriptures, and Scriptures create the message that God intended for His believers to know and use in everyday life.

In addition to reading *Spirit Seek,* word find puzzles are matched with each chapter to create an engaging, and interactive mind-stimulating experience. These puzzles are an easy way to learn Bible Scriptures that are specific to your need. The **bold** and underlined words within the Scriptures can be found in the word find puzzles. If you need "peace," *Spirit Seek* will help you find some of the Scriptures associated with that particular word – which makes *Spirit Seek* very unique!

God's love is no mystery. Exercise your desire to meditate on the Scriptures, and enjoy your spiritual journey with *Spirit Seek.*

~~ GLORY TO GOD ~~

Words can be found forward, backward, and diagonally.

Let the words of my mouth and the meditation of my heart be acceptable in Your sight, O LORD, my strength and my Redeemer.
Psalm 19:14 (NKJV)
~~~~~~~~~~~~~~~~~~~~~~~~~

~~~~ *The Old Testament* ~~~~

The Books contained within the Old Testament of the Bible reveal the covenant that God made for humanity before Christ. It includes the story of creation, religious laws, historical narratives, wisdom, and prophetic messages inspired by God. The Old Testament provides the foundation of why Christians serve a Living Saviour.

(Read & find the bold and underlined words)

<u>**Genesis**</u>
Exodus
Leviticus
<u>**Deuteronomy**</u>
Joshua
Judges
<u>**Ruth**</u>
1 Samuel
2 Samuel
1 <u>**Kings**</u>
2 Kings
1 Chronicles
2 Chronicles
Ezra
Nehemiah
<u>**Esther**</u>
Job
<u>**Psalms**</u>
Proverbs
<u>**Ecclesiastes**</u>
Song of Solomon
Isaiah
Jeremiah
<u>**Lamentations**</u>
Ezekiel
Daniel
<u>**Hosea**</u>
Joel
Amos
<u>**Obadiah**</u>
Jonah
Micah
Nahum
<u>**Habakkuk**</u>
Zephaniah
Haggai
Zechariah
<u>**Malachi**</u>

The Old Testament

S	E	T	S	A	I	S	E	L	C	C	E	H	B	V
M	N	V	U	D	H	A	I	D	A	B	O	G	U	D
J	D	O	O	E	C	H	W	S	G	S	H	X	C	L
M	X	E	I	U	A	D	O	O	E	P	G	U	Z	A
H	X	Q	E	T	L	C	G	A	S	N	P	N	J	M
N	S	Y	S	E	A	T	Z	A	T	D	E	U	I	Y
R	H	T	U	R	M	T	L	X	H	W	V	G	Y	K
O	W	P	A	O	M	M	N	C	E	X	S	Y	U	O
G	O	W	K	N	S	V	J	E	R	V	D	K	M	R
Y	X	C	D	O	S	H	L	L	M	C	K	K	A	Z
Y	L	T	Y	M	W	J	P	G	K	A	Y	W	O	Q
I	H	B	M	Y	L	S	M	K	B	F	L	K	G	S
G	O	B	L	U	Q	Y	I	A	U	M	M	S	E	E
K	L	D	P	C	A	G	H	P	Y	K	P	I	L	A
J	S	W	K	G	F	P	C	D	E	K	N	U	U	G

~~~~ *The New Testament* ~~~~

The Books contained within the New Testament reveal the life of Jesus Christ and His gift of salvation for all who believe in Him. It is the fulfillment of the Old Testament.

14 Just think how much more the blood of Christ will purify our consciences from sinful deeds so that we can worship the living God. For by the power of the eternal Spirit, Christ offered himself to God as a perfect sacrifice for our sins. 15 That is why he is the one who mediates a new covenant between God and people, so that all who are called can receive the eternal inheritance God has promised them. For Christ died to set them free from the penalty of the sins they had committed under that first covenant. Hebrews 9:14-15 (NLT)

(Read & find the bold and underlined words)

<u>Matthew</u>
Mark
<u>Luke</u>
John
<u>Acts</u>
Romans
1 Corinthians
2 **<u>Corinthians</u>**
Galatians
Ephesians
<u>Philippians</u>
Colossians
1 **<u>Thessalonians</u>**
2 Thessalonians

1 **<u>Timothy</u>**
2 Timothy
<u>Titus</u>
Philemon
<u>Hebrews</u>
James
1 Peter
2 **<u>Peter</u>**
1 John
2 John
3 **<u>John</u>**
Jude
<u>Revelation</u>

The New Testament

C	P	D	T	N	N	J	Y	T	I	M	O	T	H	Y
W	F	S	U	Q	S	O	V	L	N	V	H	H	W	P
C	E	D	S	M	W	H	E	B	R	E	W	S	W	K
K	M	O	N	Q	W	N	S	D	S	A	I	A	X	Z
S	M	W	A	M	K	U	N	S	H	U	D	D	F	S
D	X	Q	I	S	T	C	A	S	Q	I	U	K	U	N
W	D	I	H	I	O	L	I	J	C	T	F	E	F	F
P	G	A	T	G	O	J	P	O	H	E	G	W	A	X
O	P	S	N	N	F	X	P	M	K	V	M	T	E	A
V	W	U	I	N	D	N	I	U	L	A	K	B	M	Q
X	S	A	R	E	V	E	L	A	T	I	O	N	W	M
K	N	F	O	E	L	P	I	T	C	Z	B	G	S	S
S	P	V	C	Z	T	N	H	W	H	R	T	K	N	S
I	L	J	L	E	C	E	P	Z	Q	P	N	S	S	Z
A	K	K	T	F	W	M	P	A	A	D	N	X	Z	P

~~~~ AGAPE ~~~~

"*Jesus is the rock of my salvation, His banner over me is love…*" is a verse from a favorite Christian song – describing spiritual love, which is agape love. It is unconditional, genuine, and unselfish. God's everlasting love is revealed in His Word. Meditate on the Book of 1John 4, which shares the love of God through the death of His Son – Jesus Christ. Believers expressing spiritual love demonstrate their knowledge of God.

(Read & find the bold and underlined words)

Thou shalt not **<u>avenge</u>**, nor bear any grudge against the children of thy people, but thou shalt **<u>love</u>** thy neighbour as thyself: I *am* the Lord. *Leviticus 19:18 (KJV)*

Hear me, O Lord; for thy **<u>lovingkindness</u>** is good: turn unto me **<u>according</u>** to the multitude of thy **<u>tender</u>** mercies.
Psalm 69:16 (KJV)

For God so loved the world that He gave His only **<u>begotten</u>** Son, that whoever believes in Him should not **<u>perish</u>** but have **<u>everlasting</u>** life. *John 3:16* (NKJV)

The **<u>grace</u>** of the Lord Jesus Christ, and the love of God, and the **<u>communion</u>** of the Holy Spirit be with you all.
2 Corinthians 13:14 (NKJV)

8 Above all, love each other **<u>deeply</u>**, because love covers over a **<u>multitude</u>** of sins. 9 Offer hospitality to one another without grumbling. *1 Peter 4:8-9 (NIV)*

We know love by this, that he **<u>laid</u>** down his life for us – and we ought to lay down our lives for one another. *1 John 3:16 (NRSV)*

AGAPE

S	S	E	N	D	N	I	K	G	N	I	V	O	L	C
N	F	N	D	E	J	R	N	N	O	Y	V	Z	A	L
N	C	S	S	B	A	I	V	I	I	E	B	J	Y	T
B	I	Y	A	S	D	O	Q	T	N	B	L	X	J	V
R	G	R	M	R	H	I	D	S	U	J	M	N	S	K
O	R	D	O	S	U	J	A	A	M	A	S	D	A	E
B	A	C	I	W	P	W	J	L	M	X	T	V	Q	H
N	C	R	H	F	E	N	Z	R	O	T	E	O	X	T
A	E	J	R	H	M	H	S	E	C	G	V	Q	F	N
P	F	T	S	X	S	A	M	V	N	T	O	P	W	F
M	U	L	T	I	T	U	D	E	E	P	L	Y	W	R
O	F	P	D	O	R	N	V	N	S	G	J	Z	T	K
N	O	E	P	A	G	A	D	T	M	I	O	K	Y	L
F	O	L	F	N	C	E	Q	J	L	H	Q	W	V	W
A	F	Z	O	J	R	N	B	M	S	M	Q	R	X	L

~~~~ ABUNDANCE ~~~~

God is the creator and the provider of all things. Have you ever taken credit for all that you have acquired in life – knowing that it would not have been possible without the blessings from God? Give Him all of the honor and glory for the abundance in your life.

(Read & find the bold and underlined words)

But the meek shall **<u>inherit</u>** the earth; and shall **<u>delight</u>** themselves in the **<u>abundance</u>** of peace. *Psalm 37:11 (KJV)*

Now all glory to God, who is able, through his mighty power at work **<u>within</u>** us, to accomplish **<u>infinitely</u>** more than we might ask or think. *Ephesians 3:20 (NLT)*

And he said unto them, Take heed, and beware of **<u>covetousness</u>**: for a man's life consisteth not in the abundance of the things which he **<u>possesseth</u>**. *Luke 12:15 (KJV)*

13 For I do not mean that others should be eased and you
<u>burdened</u>; 14 but by an equality, that now at this time your
abundance may **<u>supply</u>** their lack, that their abundance also may
supply your lack—that there may be **<u>equality</u>**.
2 Corinthians 8:13-14 (NKJV)

16 And the gift is not like that which came through the one who
sinned. For the judgment which came from one offense resulted in
<u>condemnation</u>, but the free gift which came from many offenses
resulted in justification. 17 For if by the one man's offense death
<u>reigned</u> through the one, much more those who receive abundance
of grace and of the gift of righteousness will reign in life through
the One, Jesus Christ. *Romans 5:16-17 (NKJV)*

ABUNDANCE

N	O	I	T	A	N	M	E	D	N	O	C	Z	K	V
A	B	U	N	D	A	N	C	E	C	O	B	M	X	S
Z	B	D	Z	F	T	K	R	Z	V	X	C	L	D	Q
P	W	I	T	H	I	N	H	E	R	I	T	E	E	W
P	K	Q	E	L	S	N	T	M	D	E	C	N	G	B
E	M	R	P	R	F	O	I	E	A	J	Z	H	V	B
E	Y	L	P	P	U	S	N	T	R	X	Y	T	S	A
R	L	P	O	S	S	E	S	S	E	T	H	J	N	O
J	X	M	N	M	D	T	H	G	I	L	E	D	L	P
F	R	E	Q	R	O	R	O	L	G	I	Y	N	P	L
T	S	R	U	K	X	G	A	P	N	L	C	Z	V	D
S	X	B	H	X	O	U	X	Q	E	G	I	G	V	X
G	B	M	R	Y	Q	W	T	Z	D	E	J	F	A	U
E	C	Q	Z	E	V	T	Y	C	W	F	Y	F	Q	W
G	E	T	Q	F	B	T	T	S	Z	E	K	B	M	J

~~~~ *BELIEVE* ~~~~

The assurance of God's promise means that believers will never have to doubt the Creator. The Scriptures instruct us to confess our belief in Christ. His word should abide within our hearts at all times. Believing and trusting in God strengthens your faith and spirit - then you become a living witness to those who don't know the almighty God you serve.

(Read & find the bold and underlined words)

1 Let not your heart be troubled: ye believe in God, believe also in
me. 2 In my Father's **<u>house</u>** are many **<u>mansions</u>**: if it were not so, I
would have told you. I go to **<u>prepare</u>** a place for you.
John 14:1-2 (KJV)

9 That if thou shalt **<u>confess</u>** with thy mouth the Lord Jesus, and
shalt **<u>believe</u>** in thine heart that God hath **<u>raised</u>** him from the
dead, thou shalt be saved. 10 For with the heart man believeth unto
righteousness; and with the mouth confession is made unto
salvation. 11 For the **<u>scripture</u>** saith, Whosoever believeth on him
shall not be **<u>ashamed</u>**. *Romans 10:9-11 (KJV)*

Whoever believes and is **<u>baptized</u>** will be saved, but whoever does not believe will be **<u>condemned</u>**. *Mark 16:16 (NIV)*

'If you can'?" said Jesus. "**<u>Everything</u>** is possible for him who believes." *Mark 9:23(NIV)*

44 Then Jesus **<u>cried</u>** out, "When a man believes in me, he does not
believe in me only, but in the one who sent me. 45 When he looks
at me, he sees the one who sent me. 46 I have come into the **<u>world</u>**
as a light, so that no one who believes in me should stay in
darkness. *John 12:44-46 (NIV)*

BELIEVE

D	E	Z	I	T	P	A	B	R	G	D	H	I	E	N
E	R	U	T	P	I	R	C	S	S	E	F	N	O	C
N	Y	A	R	H	A	P	E	F	Y	Y	L	N	D	P
M	A	N	S	I	O	N	S	P	I	R	M	E	C	R
E	U	K	S	H	H	U	X	G	A	Q	I	B	U	D
D	N	E	P	G	A	I	S	R	M	R	P	V	A	G
N	D	L	J	M	V	M	B	E	C	H	E	U	N	N
O	E	L	P	R	N	S	E	G	T	T	G	I	O	H
C	Q	W	B	W	O	R	L	D	K	F	H	Q	F	P
L	J	P	D	H	O	X	I	E	Z	T	N	X	H	L
S	X	I	J	S	Q	A	E	K	Y	G	E	C	X	B
O	U	W	Z	E	A	U	V	R	O	V	C	B	R	V
Y	I	F	M	R	P	A	E	J	N	P	X	S	V	F
L	O	M	B	F	T	V	F	S	Q	K	V	C	S	C
T	V	B	R	S	E	V	O	P	E	H	G	W	G	W

~~~~ *BLESS* ~~~~

Blessings from God bring peace in your life. Because of His daily blessing, the Lord is worthy of our praise. Acknowledge and worship the Lord by sharing and demonstrating that you care. Be a blessing to others and witness the transformation in their life.

(Read & find the bold and underlined words)

The LORD will give strength unto his **<u>people</u>**; the LORD will bless his people with **<u>peace</u>**. *Psalm 29:11 (KJV)*

O **<u>taste</u>** and see that the LORD is good: blessed is the man that **<u>trusteth</u>** in him. *Psalm 34:8 (KJV)*

God blessed them and said to them, "Be fruitful and **<u>increase</u>** in number; fill the **<u>earth</u>** and **<u>subdue</u>** it. Rule over the fish of the sea and the **<u>birds</u>** of the air and over every living creature that moves on the ground." *Genesis 1:28 (NIV)*

3 Praise be to the God and Father of our Lord Jesus Christ, who has
blessed us in the heavenly realms with every spiritual blessing in
Christ. 4 For he **<u>chose</u>** us in him before the creation of the world to
be holy and **<u>blameless</u>** in his sight. *Ephesians 1:3-4 (NIV)*

32 "Now then, my sons, listen to me; blessed are those who keep
my ways. 33 Listen to my **<u>instruction</u>** and be wise; do not ignore
it. 34 Blessed is the man who listens to me, watching **<u>daily</u>** at my
doors, waiting at my **<u>doorway</u>**. *Proverbs 8:32-34 (NIV)*

<u>Blessed</u> shall you be when you come in, and blessed shall you be when you go out. *Deuteronomy 28:6 (NRSV)*

BLESS

I	E	G	D	E	S	S	E	L	B	E	U	V	G	F
N	T	T	R	U	S	T	E	T	H	O	S	R	C	R
S	S	E	L	E	M	A	L	B	G	A	U	O	X	W
T	A	P	E	O	P	L	E	I	H	F	B	P	H	E
R	T	V	Z	V	Y	A	W	R	O	O	D	O	H	C
U	N	Y	I	L	R	R	U	D	C	I	U	M	V	A
C	O	V	I	T	B	J	L	S	D	N	E	H	E	E
T	X	A	H	N	P	S	V	T	I	R	I	Q	W	P
I	D	F	K	D	P	W	D	B	V	S	E	K	Y	J
O	P	G	L	X	P	V	Y	U	S	X	I	T	V	F
N	V	F	K	U	N	H	C	K	S	Z	S	X	H	N
Z	D	K	S	X	D	S	O	O	M	V	I	J	D	I
X	M	Q	K	H	Y	O	Y	H	L	P	E	X	R	X
E	J	C	G	W	M	R	V	Z	R	D	Z	M	T	L
B	L	K	R	W	B	H	Q	Y	H	J	D	O	X	Z

~~~~ *COMPASSION* ~~~~

Jesus Christ demonstrated the greatest example of compassion by giving His life for all who have fallen short of his glory. We should be grateful for His mercy. There is healing power from a heart that beats with compassion.

(Read & find the bold and underlined words)

32 Jesus stood still and called them, saying, 'What do you want me
to do for you?' 33 They said to him, 'Lord, let our eyes be **opened**.'
34 Moved with **compassion**, Jesus touched their eyes. Immediately
they **regained** their sight and followed him.
Matthew 20:32-34 (NRSV)

But he, being full of compassion, forgave their **iniquity**, and destroyed them not: yea, many a time turned he his anger away, and did not stir up all his **wrath**. *Psalm 78:38 (KJV)*

21 Keep yourselves in the love of God, looking for the mercy of our
Lord Jesus Christ unto **eternal** life. 22 And of some have
compassion, making a **difference**: 23 And others save with fear,
pulling them out of the fire; hating even the garment spotted by the
flesh. *Jude 1:21-23 (KJV)*

8 Finally, all of you, live in **harmony** with one another; be
sympathetic, love as brothers, be compassionate and humble. 9 Do
not repay evil with evil or insult with insult, but with blessing,
because to this you were called so that you may inherit a blessing.
1Peter 3:8-9 (NIV)

8 The LORD is gracious and merciful, slow to anger and **abounding**
in **steadfast** love. 9 The LORD is good to all, and his compassion is
over all that he has made. *Psalm 145:8-9 (NRSV)*

COMPASSION

S	Q	R	K	U	D	O	B	W	G	T	B	V	Z	B
Y	L	D	I	F	F	E	R	E	N	C	E	T	V	H
M	Q	E	D	Z	X	A	J	O	I	F	X	H	F	O
P	W	F	C	T	T	Y	I	H	D	D	X	C	A	Q
A	O	C	M	H	S	S	U	M	N	E	I	X	M	A
T	C	Y	Z	O	S	A	N	K	U	N	N	V	U	G
H	C	S	U	A	S	E	F	H	O	I	I	E	I	Y
E	P	B	P	U	Y	D	L	D	B	A	Q	T	P	C
T	T	M	A	B	N	X	A	F	A	G	U	F	V	O
I	O	E	V	T	O	C	T	V	E	E	I	B	L	A
C	I	O	R	B	M	I	E	K	W	R	T	K	W	F
V	Z	Y	A	N	R	M	C	H	I	S	Y	S	H	C
T	E	A	E	Y	A	F	K	V	C	M	L	Z	C	X
Z	Q	D	W	L	H	L	A	C	X	U	E	Q	B	F
M	C	V	Z	A	T	J	W	T	Y	N	J	X	Q	A

~~~~ DIRECTION ~~~~

The Bible provides the direction that God would have His believers to follow. There will be many situations in your life when you don't know which way to turn. It is then that you call upon the Holy Spirit - who will never mislead you. Jesus is the Way to the Father.

(Read & find the bold and underlined words)

5 Trust in the LORD with all **thine** heart; and lean not unto thine
own understanding. 6 In all thy ways **acknowledge** him, and he
shall direct thy **paths**. *Proverbs 3:5-6 (KJV)*

Now God himself and our Father, and our Lord Jesus Christ, **direct** our way unto you. *1 Thessalonians 3:11 (KJV)*

5 Thomas said to him, "Lord, we don't know where you are going,
so how can we know the way?" 6 Jesus **answered**, "I am the way
and the truth and the life. No one comes to the Father **except**
through me. *John 14:5-6 (NIV)*

I know, O LORD, that a man's life is not his own; it is not for man to direct his steps. *Jeremiah 10:23 (NIV)*

A man's heart **plans** his way, But the LORD directs his **steps**. *Proverbs 16:9 (NKJV)*

The LORD will guide you **continually**, And satisfy your soul in drought, And strengthen your bones; You shall be like a watered **garden**, And like a **spring** of water, whose waters do not fail. *Isaiah 58:11 (NKJV)*

May the Lord direct your hearts to the love of God and to the **steadfastness** of Christ. *2 Thessalonians 3:5 (NRSV)*

DIRECTION

Y	A	G	P	D	S	T	A	M	E	G	P	B	O	Q
L	C	S	G	I	U	I	X	X	A	N	F	B	U	C
L	K	H	T	R	O	P	C	R	Z	I	I	A	U	W
A	N	S	W	E	R	E	D	L	T	R	P	H	L	F
U	O	Y	H	C	P	E	C	C	Z	P	I	R	T	E
N	W	A	K	T	N	S	W	X	V	S	C	H	S	R
I	L	S	T	E	A	D	F	A	S	T	N	E	S	S
T	E	P	E	U	C	P	G	G	F	U	Z	A	P	X
N	D	D	G	C	U	J	C	P	P	Y	N	T	L	U
O	G	E	R	W	O	G	U	G	Z	E	D	T	B	P
C	E	I	U	O	L	Z	H	X	S	B	B	F	R	E
K	V	I	V	E	F	V	I	R	L	E	U	K	F	J
B	T	X	S	Y	J	D	G	I	Y	J	H	N	K	O
A	P	K	U	M	Y	U	Q	P	H	T	Y	P	Q	X
J	Z	C	C	D	L	Y	W	V	U	I	G	O	Q	E

~~~~ *ENDURANCE* ~~~~

God is forever! His sustaining power can smooth out all of rough areas of life. It is difficult to endure the challenges of life without God. Complacency or wishful thinking bears no fruit. Never give up because He will never leave you.

(Read & find the bold and underlined words)

His name shall endure for ever: his **name** shall be continued as long as the sun: and men shall be blessed in him: all **nations** shall call him blessed. *Psalm 72:17 (KJV)*

10 Therefore I endure everything for the sake of the **elect**, that they
too may obtain the salvation that is in Christ Jesus, with eternal
glory. 11 Here is a **trustworthy** saying: If we died with him, we
will also live with him; 12 if we endure, we will also reign with
him. If we disown him, he will also **disown** us; 13 if we are
faithless, he will **remain** faithful, for he cannot disown himself.
2 Timothy 2:10-13 (NIV)

For His anger is but for a **moment**, His favor is for life; Weeping may endure for a night, But joy comes in the morning. *Psalm 30:5 (NKJV)*

12 And because of the increase of **lawlessness**, the love of many
will grow cold. 13 But the one who endures to the end will be
saved. *Matthew 24:12-13 (NRSV)*

10 As an example of suffering and patience, **beloved**, take the
prophets who spoke in the name of the Lord. 11 Indeed we call
blessed those who showed **endurance**. You have heard of the
endurance of Job, and you have seen the purpose of the Lord, how
the Lord is compassionate and **merciful**. *James 5:10-11 (NRSV)*

ENDURANCE

O	D	I	A	J	R	H	I	N	Z	L	J	R	G	U
H	I	N	X	U	A	L	X	Y	A	J	D	U	S	U
E	D	L	Z	Q	T	J	K	W	P	T	I	S	D	Y
G	G	U	J	X	R	B	L	V	O	X	I	R	D	E
P	R	F	G	B	U	E	E	P	U	D	N	O	D	P
U	E	I	M	C	S	L	H	L	Z	W	K	J	N	S
J	B	C	V	S	T	E	H	P	O	R	P	I	N	S
D	S	R	N	N	W	C	Q	S	F	V	C	N	S	S
W	I	E	E	A	O	T	I	O	Q	K	E	K	I	P
M	S	M	G	M	R	D	J	N	E	P	P	D	I	H
S	O	A	G	E	T	U	F	P	P	C	M	H	Q	K
M	J	I	T	I	H	X	D	V	K	R	D	P	A	Q
C	A	N	I	M	Y	A	L	N	I	N	Z	T	Z	P
T	H	N	M	L	K	Y	Q	D	E	H	H	I	E	O
A	J	J	C	G	J	Z	X	R	J	Y	H	X	A	M

~~~~ *EVERLASTING* ~~~~

There is a song that reminds you to "*build your hopes on things eternal - hold to God's unchanging hand.*" If our hope is in the Lord, we are guaranteed that His Word is everlasting.

(Read & find the bold and underlined words)

For he that soweth to his flesh shall of the **flesh** reap corruption; but he that **soweth** to the Spirit shall of the Spirit reap life everlasting. *Galatians 6:8 (KJV)*

Whenever the **rainbow** appears in the clouds, I will see it and remember the everlasting **covenant** between God and all living **creatures** of every kind on the earth." *Genesis 9:16 (KJV)*

For God so loved the world, that he gave his only **begotten** Son, that whosoever believeth in him should not **perish**, but have everlasting life. *John 3:16 (KJV)*

For the LORD is good; His mercy is everlasting, And His truth endures to all **generations**. *Psalm 100:5 (NKJV)*

39 This is the will of the Father who sent Me, that of all He has
given Me I should lose nothing, but should **raise** it up at the last
day. 40 And this is the will of Him who sent Me, that **everyone**
who sees the Son and believes in Him may have everlasting life;
and I will raise him up at the last day." *John 6:39-40 (NKJV)*

For to us a child is born,
  to us a son is given,
  and the government will be on his **shoulders**.
  And he will be called
  Wonderful Counselor, Mighty God,
  Everlasting Father, Prince of Peace. *Isaiah 9:6 (NIV)*

EVERLASTING

E	S	L	I	H	X	D	G	Q	P	I	Z	Q	Y	Y
V	H	Q	K	X	Q	O	F	E	E	E	C	Q	O	P
E	O	T	K	X	S	D	T	Q	M	X	N	E	U	C
R	U	N	N	E	U	K	P	U	A	I	Y	L	C	V
L	L	N	S	A	F	G	E	E	O	R	E	F	M	F
A	D	U	Q	I	N	B	V	C	R	A	Z	L	I	R
S	E	R	U	T	A	E	R	C	K	I	I	E	X	K
T	R	W	E	T	R	G	V	D	P	S	S	S	H	Y
I	S	O	F	Y	S	O	S	O	W	E	T	H	J	O
N	H	B	O	W	U	T	A	W	C	P	T	I	A	I
G	E	N	E	R	A	T	I	O	N	S	X	R	G	S
T	E	I	K	W	V	E	O	Y	Q	F	A	T	D	R
T	J	A	F	O	V	N	X	U	D	S	U	X	K	Y
R	C	R	I	G	P	O	Z	G	U	O	J	W	B	C
T	U	F	T	C	F	H	O	E	H	J	K	Q	N	E

~~~~ *EXCELLENT* ~~~~

Mediocrity could never be associated with the Almighty God. The beauty of nature, the activity of our limbs, the oxygen that keeps us alive - are all in God's perfect will. Following His example enables us to carryout our lives in an excellent manner. The pursuit of excellence is not an easy mission for most people, but the outcome is worth the journey.

(Read & find the bold and underlined words)

For wisdom is a defence, and **money** is a defence: but the **excellency** of knowledge is, that wisdom giveth life to them that have it. *Ecclesiastes 7:12 (KJV)*

Touching the Almighty, we cannot find him out: he is excellent in power, and in judgment, and in **plenty** of justice: he will not afflict. *Job 37:23 (KJV)*

He that hath knowledge **spareth** his words: and a man of understanding is of an excellent spirit. *Proverbs 17:27 (KJV)*

Soon **Daniel** **distinguished** himself above all the other presidents and **satraps** because an excellent spirit was in him, and the king planned to appoint him over the **whole** kingdom. *Daniel 6:3 (NRSV)*

But **strive** for the **greater** gifts. And I will show you a still more excellent way. *1 Corinthians 12:31 (NRSV)*

O LORD, our Lord, How excellent is Your name in all the **earth**, Who have set Your glory above the heavens! *Psalm 8:1 (NKJV)*

EXCELLENT

B	S	E	S	D	G	T	W	W	V	V	B	D	R	O
J	C	R	P	O	T	C	J	U	H	P	I	T	I	A
S	E	A	A	M	F	E	D	N	F	S	C	Y	I	O
X	V	F	R	G	Y	R	V	A	T	Y	O	J	G	O
Y	Y	E	T	O	U	C	H	I	N	G	G	T	X	E
P	Y	Y	A	W	W	O	N	D	R	I	J	Z	Z	A
G	W	V	S	J	H	G	R	E	A	T	E	R	A	V
T	U	E	G	P	U	O	R	P	L	S	S	L	A	S
R	E	R	Z	I	A	X	L	L	E	L	M	V	X	V
P	N	W	S	H	T	R	A	E	V	Y	E	O	F	X
S	P	H	I	D	B	Y	E	N	O	M	Z	C	P	J
R	E	Z	N	K	M	C	W	T	X	L	O	T	X	D
D	J	I	U	Q	E	Z	W	Y	H	U	Z	Y	Q	E
X	D	Y	S	B	Q	Q	S	B	B	C	D	U	V	B
N	N	Y	K	A	O	E	S	E	V	Z	Y	Y	M	W

~~~~ *FAITH* ~~~~

It is only human to question our faith when various situations in our life take an unexpected turn. No matter what the circumstances are, God is the true source of our faith. The Holy Spirit is the greatest comforter that we can depend on while on earth. Our challenge is to learn patience, and wait on the Lord.

(Read & find the bold and underlined words)

Looking unto Jesus the author and **finisher** of our faith; who for the joy that was set before him endured the cross, despising the shame, and is set down at the right hand of the **throne** of God. *Hebrews 12:2 (KJV)*

Now faith is the **substance** of things hoped for, the **evidence** of things not seen. *Hebrews 11:1 (K JV)*

21 But now a righteousness from God, apart from law, has been
made known, to which the Law and the Prophets **testify**. 22 This
righteousness from God comes through faith in Jesus Christ to all
who believe. There is no difference, 23 for all have **sinned** and fall
short of the glory of God, 24 and are **justified** freely by his grace
through the **redemption** that came by Christ Jesus.
Romans 3:21-24 (NIV)

For just as the body without the spirit is dead, so faith **without** works is also dead. *James 2:26 (NRSV)*

He said to them, "Because of your little faith. For truly I tell you, if you have faith the size of a **mustard** seed, you will say to this **mountain**, 'Move from here to there,' and it will move; and nothing will be **impossible** for you." *Matthew 17:20 (NRSV)*

FAITH

R	H	U	P	Y	F	P	Q	K	E	K	E	C	H	M
L	Y	W	M	N	O	P	L	L	I	B	A	B	G	N
S	R	W	J	S	O	T	B	J	H	L	R	Y	F	E
Y	J	E	Z	U	B	I	F	L	K	M	R	P	H	R
H	I	M	H	B	S	Q	T	U	O	H	T	I	W	Z
Y	F	I	T	S	E	T	V	P	Y	O	M	S	X	E
Y	F	K	O	T	I	S	I	Q	M	T	K	N	V	U
K	L	P	M	A	Z	N	G	F	A	E	H	I	E	W
J	M	O	U	N	T	A	I	N	I	J	D	Y	N	R
I	G	P	S	C	E	Z	G	F	J	E	D	E	O	G
W	B	G	T	E	E	S	I	N	N	E	D	C	R	Z
Q	G	F	A	U	L	U	F	C	T	A	P	Y	H	J
I	O	S	R	K	C	V	E	A	L	N	J	S	T	D
V	K	K	D	U	V	W	F	P	F	V	O	M	T	W
C	V	Q	K	N	E	U	Z	D	O	E	K	Y	N	M

~~~~ *FELLOWSHIP* ~~~~

Your relationship with Christ, family, and friends is important for building God's kingdom. There are a multitude of opportunities to commune with one another – like serving on a ministry team, sharing a meal, or attending worship service. As Christians, we are called to be in fellowship with Christ and all of His children from all walks of life.

(Read & find the bold and underlined words)

God is **<u>faithful</u>**, by whom ye were called unto the **<u>fellowship</u>** of his Son Jesus Christ our Lord. *1 Corinthians 1:9 (KJV)*

Do not be **<u>yoked</u>** together with unbelievers. For what do righteousness and **<u>wickedness</u>** have in **<u>common</u>**? Or what fellowship can light have with darkness? *2 Corinthians 6:14 (NIV)*

41 Then those who **<u>gladly</u>** received his word were baptized; and that day about three **<u>thousand</u>** souls were added to them. 42 And they continued **<u>steadfastly</u>** in the apostles' **<u>doctrine</u>** and fellowship, in the breaking of **<u>bread</u>**, and in prayers. *Acts 2:41-42 (NKJV)*

All things came into being **<u>through</u>** him, and without him not one thing came into being. *John 1:3 (NRSV)*

...we **<u>declare</u>** to you what we have seen and **<u>heard</u>** so that you also may have fellowship with us; and truly our fellowship is with the Father and with his Son Jesus Christ. *1 John 1:3 (NRSV)*

FELLOWSHIP

W	N	O	O	G	N	T	X	S	P	V	H	D	R	S
S	S	E	N	D	E	K	C	I	W	I	R	G	B	G
L	W	P	R	F	M	R	H	Z	Q	K	H	J	U	G
U	W	A	D	R	E	S	Z	D	D	G	J	I	K	U
F	E	E	I	F	W	I	R	E	U	L	V	Y	D	T
H	K	V	N	O	G	B	C	O	M	M	O	N	O	L
T	X	L	L	W	T	L	R	H	M	K	U	U	H	K
I	A	L	W	G	A	H	A	E	E	Y	L	D	P	Z
A	E	N	I	R	T	C	O	D	A	I	J	B	B	G
F	D	A	E	U	K	V	T	U	L	D	R	L	X	U
D	F	I	Y	C	W	T	M	M	S	Y	D	T	U	T
F	G	K	Y	L	T	S	A	F	D	A	E	T	S	U
H	J	H	G	I	P	Q	I	G	M	O	N	O	L	N
P	J	R	U	A	X	U	B	Z	W	Y	N	D	Z	I
U	A	T	O	U	K	A	I	W	S	Z	K	I	O	I

~~~~ *FORGIVENESS* ~~~~

The act of forgiveness can be a bitter pill to swallow when you have been deeply hurt by another person. The pain residing within the victim can be unbearable. Knowing that the blood of Jesus washed away our sins, we must learn to forgive and ask God to release the pain – that is healing!

(Read & find the bold and underlined words)

31 Wherefore I say unto you, All **manner** of sin and blasphemy
shall be **forgiven** unto men: but the **blasphemy** against the Holy
Ghost shall not be forgiven unto men. 32 And whosoever speaketh
a word against the Son of man, it shall be forgiven him: but whosoever speaketh against the Holy **Ghost**, it shall not be forgiven him, neither in this world, neither in the world to come. *Matthew 12:31-32 (KJV)*

31 Get rid of all **bitterness**, rage and anger, brawling and **slander**,
along with every form of **malice**. 32 Be kind and compassionate to
one another, forgiving each other, just as in Christ God **forgave** you. *Ephesians 4:31-32 (NIV)*

25 "And whenever you stand **praying**, if you have **anything**
against anyone, forgive him, that your Father in heaven may also
forgive you your trespasses. 26 But if you do not forgive, neither
will your Father in heaven forgive your **trespasses**." *Mark 11:25-26 (NKJV)*

Peter said to them, "Repent, and be baptized every one of you in the name of Jesus Christ so that your sins may be forgiven; and you will **receive** the gift of the Holy Spirit. *Acts 2:38 (NRSV)*

FORGIVENESS

T	R	E	S	P	A	S	S	E	S	B	A	K	B	Q
R	V	Z	X	Y	W	N	V	C	L	R	W	T	Y	I
E	M	I	J	E	B	A	Y	A	E	S	K	S	F	U
S	Q	X	J	R	G	R	S	T	N	G	M	O	B	T
Y	R	N	D	R	L	P	E	Q	H	M	G	H	Z	B
H	R	U	O	G	H	P	R	A	Y	I	N	G	O	Y
P	K	F	G	E	E	U	U	E	V	I	N	Y	S	T
D	Q	E	M	Z	V	U	X	E	C	D	U	G	A	Y
Y	C	Y	O	M	L	I	N	Z	U	I	N	Q	E	R
M	Z	I	F	H	G	R	E	D	N	A	L	S	Z	B
Z	Q	I	W	W	I	K	Z	C	L	K	D	A	Y	Q
P	K	B	C	W	I	P	H	R	E	N	N	A	M	T
Y	J	B	J	G	B	I	T	T	E	R	N	E	S	S
Q	T	M	P	B	V	B	G	K	Y	Z	W	D	P	V
Q	Z	Z	V	Y	O	W	U	H	U	X	U	X	U	U

~~~~ *FREE* ~~~~

The unrestrained, liberating free will in Jesus Christ has been given to believers through the Holy Spirit. To be free in Christ means that you are covered - at no cost - by His anointing spirit. Discover who you are in Jesus Christ and give thanks for what He has done for you.

(Read & find the bold and underlined words)

<u>Restore</u> unto me the joy of thy salvation; and **<u>uphold</u>** me with thy free spirit. *Psalm 51:12 (KJV)*

17 But thanks be to God that, though you used to be slaves to sin,
you **<u>wholeheartedly</u>** obeyed the form of teaching to which you
were **<u>entrusted</u>**. 18 You have been set **<u>free</u>** from sin and have
become slaves to righteousness. *Romans 6:17-18 (NIV)*

34 **<u>Jesus</u>** answered them, "Most **<u>assuredly</u>**, I say to you, whoever
commits sin is a slave of sin. 35 And a slave does not abide in the
house forever, but a son **<u>abides</u>** forever. 36 Therefore if the Son
makes you free, you shall be free **<u>indeed</u>**. *John 8:34-36 (NKJV)*

Stand fast therefore in the **<u>liberty</u>** by which Christ has made us free, and do not be **<u>entangled</u>** again with a yoke of **<u>bondage</u>**. *Galatians 5:1 (NKJV)*

FREE

W	U	D	B	D	V	M	G	B	T	Y	B	U	L	Z
Y	H	J	E	S	A	C	S	N	J	J	A	L	X	Y
Y	C	O	X	T	G	M	Q	K	F	S	X	I	Q	M
L	R	Z	L	K	S	Z	K	M	S	V	U	B	W	V
Z	K	E	W	E	W	U	Q	U	J	E	P	S	A	A
Y	K	R	G	P	H	A	R	T	N	S	H	Q	E	A
S	L	O	W	A	P	E	I	T	Y	B	O	T	B	J
M	Z	T	L	S	D	A	B	U	N	R	L	B	F	Z
Y	P	S	T	L	J	N	B	R	S	E	D	R	M	W
T	T	E	Y	U	G	N	O	D	T	H	E	N	V	G
K	A	R	H	L	D	V	D	B	Q	E	E	G	C	O
J	Z	M	E	F	M	T	N	O	B	C	D	U	Q	N
S	E	D	I	B	A	M	D	R	K	Y	N	L	S	H
M	M	W	F	I	I	H	E	Q	B	M	I	C	Y	Q
U	X	I	L	W	I	L	W	I	Q	R	X	P	H	L

~~~~ FRIEND ~~~~

There are so many levels of friendship. It has been often quoted that "to have friends, you must be a friend." What does that take? Try honesty, sacrifice, dependability, responsibility, caring, sharing and loyalty - among other attributes. It is without doubt that we have a true friend in Jesus Christ. Consider the impact on the world if we exercised our ability to become true friends.

(Read & find the bold and underlined words)

Iron sharpeneth iron; so a man **sharpeneth** the **countenance** of his friend. *Proverbs 27:17 (KJV)*

A man who has friends must himself be **friendly**, But there is a friend who **sticks** closer than a **brother**. *Proverbs 18:24 (NKJV)*

And the **LORD** restored Job's losses when he prayed for his friends. Indeed the LORD gave Job **twice** as much as he had before. *Job 42:10 (NKJV)*

But Jesus **refused**, and said to him, "Go **home** to your friends, and tell them how much the Lord has done for you, and what mercy he has shown you." *Mark 5:19 (NRSV)*

A friend loves at all times, and **kinsfolk** are born to share **adversity**. *Proverbs 17:17 (NSRV)*

FRIEND

S	J	R	X	R	Y	T	Z	H	H	E	B	G	I	S
K	H	T	B	L	T	T	H	S	C	O	R	R	I	E
C	O	A	P	E	I	K	I	N	S	F	O	L	K	G
I	M	O	R	H	S	F	A	K	R	N	T	O	C	H
T	E	K	H	P	R	N	O	I	L	F	H	F	M	Z
S	K	L	J	G	E	R	E	F	U	S	E	D	P	P
E	C	I	W	T	V	N	F	T	X	W	R	H	S	I
M	D	D	N	V	D	L	E	O	X	O	I	W	H	K
U	X	U	R	L	A	W	E	T	L	X	V	F	Y	O
P	O	I	Y	N	G	Q	W	Q	H	T	K	E	R	R
C	T	P	H	B	M	T	C	D	C	I	D	S	O	B
D	W	R	S	H	D	V	P	T	E	S	M	U	A	D
F	F	C	A	C	L	P	H	P	Z	V	B	U	E	H
J	S	T	E	O	R	Z	O	B	A	C	H	S	R	M
F	F	J	V	Y	U	A	Z	B	H	X	X	Y	Q	V

~~~~ *FRUITFUL* ~~~~

Believers in Christ Jesus are witnesses of the fruits produced by God. Examine the manner and methods of bringing forth fruit that glorifies God? When we serve and bless others, the outgrowth will appear from God. The best way to begin is with love.

(Read & find the bold and underlined words)

And God blessed them, saying, Be **fruitful**, and **multiply**, and fill the **waters** in the seas, and let fowl multiply in the earth. *Genesis 1:22 (KJV)*

And we pray this in **order** that you may live a life **worthy** of the Lord and may please him in every way: **bearing** fruit in every good work, **growing** in the knowledge of God… *Colossians 1:10 (NIV)*

15 "Beware of **false** prophets, who come to you in sheep's clothing,
but **inwardly** they are **ravenous** wolves. 16 You will know them by
their fruits. Do men gather grapes from thornbushes or figs from
thistles? 17 Even so, every good tree bears good fruit, but a bad tree
bears bad fruit. *Matthew 7:15-17 (NKJV)*

4 Abide in me as I abide in you. Just as the **branch** cannot bear
fruit by itself unless it abides in the vine, neither can you unless
you abide in me. 5 I am the vine, you are the branches. Those who
abide in me and I in them bear much fruit, because apart from me
you can do nothing. *John 15:4-5 (NRSV)*

He is like a tree planted by **streams** of water, which **yields** its fruit in **season** and whose leaf does not wither. Whatever he does prospers. *Psalm 1:3 (NIV)*

FRUITFUL

L	Y	V	I	H	T	S	X	M	V	U	P	O	J	B
K	U	J	Q	R	S	V	U	J	O	T	X	S	Z	B
G	W	F	E	I	D	L	X	O	M	I	E	V	K	P
X	O	D	T	V	T	P	H	C	N	A	R	B	G	H
G	R	O	W	I	N	G	E	W	S	E	X	S	H	B
O	T	S	P	D	U	S	A	O	F	D	V	M	E	O
G	H	L	O	V	Z	R	N	Y	E	S	L	A	F	P
P	Y	M	U	L	D	E	F	K	W	K	R	E	R	X
Q	D	E	Z	L	M	T	R	G	J	I	Y	R	I	C
R	A	P	Y	T	Q	A	B	B	N	F	E	T	I	Y
M	U	I	V	E	V	W	S	G	L	P	S	S	U	E
J	J	Z	K	Q	U	S	S	I	J	C	E	A	M	G
V	Z	K	E	D	U	U	V	Q	F	V	I	D	D	A
H	G	N	L	F	N	K	Q	A	N	Z	R	D	R	Q
Q	B	W	Z	C	C	Z	X	E	L	N	L	B	N	W

~~~~ *GIFT* ~~~~

The Scriptures reveal that there is no greater gift than eternal life. The material things given from your salary are not gifts - it is what comes from the goodness of your heart. Gifts can also be special talents that set you apart. As it is often stated – you must use it or you'll lose it. Share your gifts!

(Read & find the bold and underlined words)

For the **<u>wages</u>** of sin is death; but the gift of God is eternal life through Jesus Christ our Lord. *Romans 6:23 (KJV)*

Every good gift and every **<u>perfect</u>** gift is from above, and cometh down from the Father of lights, with whom is no **<u>variableness</u>**, neither shadow of turning. *James 1:17 (KJV)*

As each one has received a gift, minister it to one another, as good **<u>stewards</u>** of the **<u>manifold</u>** grace of God. *1 Peter 4:10 (NKJV)*

I wish that all were as I myself am. But each has a **<u>particular</u>** gift from God, one having one kind and another a different kind. *1 Corinthians 7:7 (NRSV)*

Jesus **<u>answered</u>** her, "If you knew the gift of God, and who it is that is saying to you, 'Give me a drink,' you would have asked him, and he would have given you living water." *John 4:10 (NRSV)*

11 The **<u>gifts</u>** he gave were that some would be apostles, some
prophets, some **<u>evangelists</u>**, some pastors and teachers, 12 to equip
the **<u>saints</u>** for the work of ministry, for building up the body of
Christ, 13 until all of us come to the unity of the faith and of the
knowledge of the Son of God, to **<u>maturity</u>**, to the measure of the
full **<u>stature</u>** of Christ. *Ephesians 4:11-13 (NRSV)*

GIFT

E	P	A	R	T	I	C	U	L	A	R	L	L	N	M
V	U	N	V	D	C	E	L	D	Z	U	L	Y	F	L
A	X	S	S	E	N	E	L	B	A	I	R	A	V	F
N	N	W	Q	K	T	E	F	O	Y	U	Z	S	Y	V
G	J	E	F	D	P	O	F	R	F	B	T	V	I	Q
E	L	R	F	Y	S	Y	Z	S	E	E	Y	Z	K	D
L	O	E	P	I	T	I	S	T	W	P	Y	R	F	E
I	R	D	L	O	F	I	N	A	M	Z	D	E	R	S
S	Y	S	E	N	I	Y	R	T	U	W	H	H	Q	L
T	T	C	D	C	G	D	H	U	D	P	O	N	D	Z
S	T	N	I	A	S	R	T	R	T	A	L	S	U	I
V	D	Z	T	K	D	T	S	E	G	A	W	C	F	T
N	Z	I	A	A	Z	I	U	R	H	W	M	C	U	P
O	J	J	J	A	E	E	I	Z	Q	W	W	G	G	P
Y	G	F	V	D	G	T	F	V	D	U	Z	R	G	L

~~~~ *GIVING* ~~~~

God gives life when we wake up from a deep sleep. He supplies every need that we might have according to His will. Take joy in giving just as God gives to us. It could mean a monetary donation to a charity, ministry, or scholarship fund. Giving also means time well spent with others. Selfishness serves no one, but even the smallest act of giving can change the lives of many.

(Read & find the bold and underlined words)

Each man should give what he has decided in his heart to give, not reluctantly or under **compulsion**, for God loves a **cheerful** giver. *2 Corinthians 9:7 (NIV)*

Delight yourself also in the LORD, And He shall give you the desires of your heart. *Psalm 37:4 (NKJV)*

It is the Spirit who gives life; the flesh **profits** nothing. The words that I speak to you are spirit, and they are life. *John 6:63 (NKJV)*

17 As for those who in the present age are rich, command them not
to be haughty, or to set their hopes on the **uncertainty** of **riches**,
but rather on God who richly provides us with everything for our
enjoyment. 18 They are to do good, to be rich in good works,
generous, and ready to share, 19 thus storing up for themselves the
treasure of a good **foundation** for the future, so that they may
take hold of the life that really is life. *1 Timothy 6:17-19 (NRSV)*

If it is **encouraging**, let him encourage; if it is **contributing** to the needs of others, let him give generously; if it is leadership, let him govern **diligently**; if it is showing mercy, let him do it cheerfully. *Romans 12:8 (NIV)*

GIVING

G	N	I	T	U	B	I	R	T	N	O	C	F	C	A
U	N	C	E	R	T	A	I	N	T	Y	R	M	P	S
U	R	I	C	H	E	S	A	L	L	C	M	L	U	T
N	H	G	G	H	U	Q	H	T	O	S	S	P	F	T
I	C	R	H	A	E	Z	N	M	U	T	L	O	R	T
D	N	G	V	U	R	E	P	O	I	V	Y	E	Z	T
R	O	W	D	F	G	U	R	F	R	F	A	B	S	N
I	I	I	E	I	L	E	O	F	D	S	O	M	Y	E
V	T	C	L	S	N	R	U	C	U	S	I	B	L	V
W	A	I	I	E	P	F	R	R	N	L	C	U	P	Q
Z	D	O	G	E	S	B	E	J	Z	E	H	V	T	S
U	N	K	H	F	W	S	I	L	V	U	E	J	U	Q
K	U	G	T	O	I	M	E	G	U	I	H	S	W	Z
L	O	Q	A	I	T	E	K	Q	Q	A	R	V	S	C
W	F	Q	M	V	R	O	Y	P	D	I	U	D	F	W

~~~~ *GRACE* ~~~~

What an awesome feeling it is to know that you are the receiver of God's grace. We are often told that His grace is sufficient. This implies that it is enough to get us through any circumstance that we encounter according to His will.

(Read & find the bold and underlined words)

For the LORD God is a sun and **<u>shield</u>**: the LORD will give grace and glory: no good thing will he withhold from them that walk **<u>uprightly</u>**. *Psalm 84:11 (KJV)*

And the Word was made flesh, and **<u>dwelt</u>** among us, (and we beheld his glory, the glory as of the only begotten of the Father,) full of grace and truth. *John 1:14 (KJV)*

But not as the offence, so also is the free gift. For if through the offence of one many be dead, much more the grace of God, and the gift by grace, which is by one man, Jesus Christ, hath **<u>abounded</u>** unto many. *Romans 5:15 (KJV)*

You are the most excellent of men and your lips have been **<u>anointed</u>** with grace, since God has blessed you **<u>forever</u>**. *Psalm 45:2 (NIV)*

8 "Those who cling to worthless idols **<u>forfeit</u>** the grace that could be theirs. 9 But I, with a song of **<u>thanksgiving</u>**, will sacrifice to you. What I have vowed I will make good. Salvation comes from the LORD." *Jonah 2:8-9 (NIV)*

Let no corrupt word **<u>proceed</u>** out of your mouth, but what is good for necessary **<u>edification</u>**, that it may impart grace to the hearers. *Ephesians 4:29 (NKJV)*

For sin shall not have **<u>dominion</u>** over you, for you are not under law but under **<u>grace</u>**. *Romans 6:14 (NKJV)*

GRACE

G	M	N	A	S	K	B	T	K	N	C	Q	T	S	M
A	N	O	I	N	T	E	D	A	E	H	T	Z	J	R
K	T	I	E	F	R	O	F	C	D	C	U	K	S	K
Y	G	T	V	X	M	H	A	T	C	O	F	S	O	C
K	N	A	L	I	W	R	Q	A	V	D	Q	Q	Q	I
L	P	C	N	E	G	I	T	J	P	U	F	G	V	K
C	R	I	L	S	W	S	E	S	L	U	A	F	D	M
T	O	F	X	J	C	D	K	G	H	S	B	V	U	B
N	C	I	E	Y	N	W	F	N	X	I	N	W	B	O
D	E	D	E	D	N	U	O	B	A	Q	E	M	R	M
E	E	E	Z	M	U	P	R	I	G	H	T	L	Y	L
T	D	Z	V	D	D	Z	E	L	C	B	T	J	D	V
Y	H	Q	T	X	U	K	V	O	X	D	W	G	U	R
J	K	G	L	C	K	A	E	O	Q	C	E	V	G	R
Y	L	J	Q	P	P	F	R	B	I	R	G	S	C	A

~~~~ *GROW* ~~~~

Taking time to expand our knowledge of God is an act of spiritual growth. The greatest opportunity to know God is by studying the Bible. We also grow and learn about life from our parents or other family members; and we educate ourselves by attending various learning institutions. Spiritual growth is a process that doesn't happen overnight – yet; it will take you much further along life's journey.

(Read & find the bold and underlined words)

But **grow** in grace, and in the knowledge of our Lord and **Saviour** Jesus Christ. To him be glory both now and for ever. Amen. *2 Peter 3:18 (KJV)*

Nevertheless, the righteous will hold to their ways, and those with clean hands will grow **stronger**. *Job 17:9 (NIV)*

He who **walks** with the wise grows wise, but a companion of fools **suffers** harm. *Proverbs 13:20 (NIV)*

5 What, after all, is **Apollos**? And what is **Paul**? Only servants,
through whom you came to believe—as the Lord has **assigned** to
each his task. 6 I **planted** the seed, Apollos watered it, but God
made it grow. 7 So neither he who plants nor he who waters is
anything, but only God, who makes things grow.
1 Corinthians 3:5-7 (NIV)

Like **newborn** infants, long for the pure, spiritual milk, so that by
it you may grow into salvation – 3 if indeed you have **tasted** that
the Lord is good. *1 Peter 2:2-3 (NRSV)*

GROW

S	Q	U	U	S	H	C	C	P	P	X	R	S	I	G
Q	S	R	K	G	R	O	W	A	L	K	S	S	G	M
C	D	E	N	G	I	S	S	A	A	C	D	H	R	V
M	O	M	L	N	R	N	A	P	N	E	Y	U	D	F
U	P	B	R	E	G	N	O	R	T	S	I	U	Z	E
R	X	R	F	W	H	L	E	S	E	B	Z	Z	X	N
K	E	F	K	B	L	T	A	S	D	I	B	O	P	I
Z	U	Z	H	O	N	T	R	U	O	I	V	A	S	F
S	G	E	S	R	K	P	X	E	A	R	U	K	T	Z
F	E	C	Z	N	E	A	P	W	V	L	X	V	G	X
V	R	W	F	N	Q	I	J	R	H	E	Y	G	X	A
S	Z	Q	N	J	A	S	P	L	K	N	N	R	O	Y
W	V	Y	F	H	H	O	V	D	V	A	D	R	D	F
S	M	G	Z	G	F	X	K	W	W	D	P	H	H	K
E	R	L	Z	M	S	W	G	L	Z	B	T	W	K	G

~~~~ *HEART* ~~~~

The essence of character is setting one's heart on the Lord. Difficult situations may cause you much despair, but it is in the core of your heart where pain, suffering, and ultimately healing reside. The heart is one of the most fragile parts of the body. Give your heart to Christ - for He alone is the best one to handle the desires and pains in your heart.

(Read & find the bold and underlined words)

"Blessed are the pure in **heart**, for they will see God. *Matthew 5:8 (NRSV)*

Wait on the LORD: be of good **courage**, and he shall strengthen thine heart: wait, I say, on the LORD. *Psalm 27:14 (KJV)*

8 So God, who knows the heart, **acknowledged** them by giving
them the Holy Spirit, just as He did to us, 9 and made no
distinction between us and them, **purifying** their hearts by faith.
Acts 15:8-9 (NKJV)

5 You shall love the LORD your God with all your heart, with all
your soul, and with all your strength. 6 "And these words which I
command you **today** shall be in your heart.
Deuteronomy 6:5-6 (NKJV)

And **Hannah** prayed and said: "My heart rejoices in the LORD; My horn is **exalted** in the LORD. I **smile** at my enemies, Because I rejoice in Your salvation. *1 Samuel 2:1 (NKJV)*

…behold, I have done according to your words; see, I have given you a wise and understanding heart, so that there has not been anyone like you before you, nor shall any like you **arise** after you. *1 Kings 3:12 (NKJV)*

Anxiety weighs down the **human** heart, but a good word cheers it up. *Proverbs 12:25 (NRSV)*

HEART

D	P	E	U	S	K	I	H	M	G	N	U	A	Y	T
E	I	Q	Z	P	M	A	A	Q	H	A	X	J	L	D
G	A	S	Q	G	N	N	X	Q	B	S	I	Q	T	A
D	T	F	T	N	X	S	E	U	V	I	I	V	X	Q
E	O	B	A	I	Q	C	X	C	H	L	W	G	K	P
L	D	H	E	Y	N	I	A	Y	U	C	P	E	O	E
W	A	T	E	F	Z	C	L	A	M	K	Y	N	H	A
O	Y	P	B	I	A	O	T	R	A	E	H	T	Y	S
N	U	K	G	R	T	U	E	I	N	W	N	A	D	P
K	D	D	P	U	P	R	D	S	O	B	Y	C	G	I
C	B	V	J	P	R	A	U	E	M	N	Y	V	C	S
A	F	M	L	U	D	G	A	W	W	I	G	K	G	O
D	P	K	Z	W	S	E	A	M	Q	W	L	L	X	X
O	S	K	G	D	C	G	W	H	R	Y	G	E	S	E
U	K	N	S	Q	G	T	Y	F	J	I	R	V	Z	C

~~~~ *HOLINESS* ~~~~

Because God is holy, it is expected that His believers become holy as well. Not in sense that one person is better than another but rather one who is Christ-like, displaying love and obedience. The Bible explains that holiness and cleanliness is next to Godliness. The life that God wants us to live is to be free from sin, which results in holiness.

(Read & find the bold and underlined words)

Sing unto the LORD, O ye saints of his, and give thanks at the **remembrance** of his **holiness**. *Psalm 30:4 (KJV)*

Because it is **written**, Be ye holy; for I am holy.
1 Peter 1:16 (KJV)

He that is **unjust**, let him be unjust still: and he which is **filthy**, let him be filthy still: and he that is righteous, let him be righteous still: and he that is holy, let him be holy still. *Revelation 22:11 (KJV)*

Regard them as holy, because they offer up the **food** of your God. **Consider** them holy, because I the LORD am holy—I who make you holy. *Leviticus 21:8 (NIV)*

Who is like You, O Lord, among the gods? Who is like You, **glorious** in holiness, **Fearful** in praises, doing **wonders**? *Exodus 15:11 (NKJV)*

HOLINESS

R	E	M	E	M	B	R	A	N	C	E	Y	I	S	A
Q	L	W	K	G	L	O	R	I	O	U	S	D	F	N
V	H	F	P	M	H	O	L	I	N	E	S	S	E	E
E	B	B	M	M	Q	U	B	O	S	F	I	T	R	T
J	M	D	U	V	O	L	U	L	I	G	N	E	D	T
D	H	A	G	R	T	G	U	L	D	A	G	R	B	I
V	R	R	P	C	M	X	T	F	E	A	C	H	A	R
D	W	M	A	V	Y	H	A	S	R	E	D	N	O	W
O	C	Z	J	V	Y	N	X	D	U	A	U	O	A	I
E	P	V	U	X	N	U	J	R	R	J	E	V	O	Q
F	E	N	S	O	I	I	G	J	V	G	N	F	A	F
O	L	E	H	D	P	S	J	Q	U	Y	D	U	C	W
V	M	J	Y	J	G	P	M	T	J	C	G	D	R	K
W	Z	J	A	Z	G	N	R	P	D	E	X	F	F	F
D	K	O	Y	T	D	Y	R	Q	Y	Q	F	J	E	X

~~~~ *HOLY SPIRIT* ~~~~

The Comforter - the third person of the Trinity (Father, Son, and Holy Spirit) - was sent by Jesus. The Holy Spirit is an advocate for believers. Listen to the silent voice that tells you right from wrong. The Holy Spirit is our 'way out of no way' and helps to guide our actions and decisions. Allow the Holy Spirit to live inside of you so that God's character can be revealed.

(Read & find the bold and underlined words)

7 For God hath not called us unto **uncleanness**, but unto holiness.
8 He therefore that **despiseth**, despiseth not man, but God, who
hath also given unto us his holy Spirit.
1 Thessalonians 4:7-8 (KJV)

Nevertheless I tell you the truth; It is **expedient** for you that I go away: for if I go not away, the **Comforter** will not come unto you; but if I depart, I will send him unto you. *John 16:7 (KJV)*

But the **Counselor**, the Holy Spirit, whom the Father will send in my name, will teach you all things and will remind you of everything I have said to you. *John 14:26 (NIV)*

For the **Kingdom** of God is not a matter of what we eat or drink, but of living a life of **goodness** and peace and joy in the Holy **Spirit**. *Romans 14:17 (NLT)*

Then Peter said to them, "Repent, and let every one of you be baptized in the name of Jesus Christ for the **remission** of sins; and you shall receive the gift of the **Holy** Spirit." *Acts 2:38 (NKJV)*

…and hope does not **disappoint** us, because God's love has been **poured** into our hearts through the Holy Spirit that has been given to us. *Romans 5:5 (NRSV)*

HOLY SPIRIT

S	S	E	N	N	A	E	L	C	N	U	E	Q	Z	M
T	N	I	O	P	P	A	S	I	D	N	X	D	R	J
R	L	K	P	C	R	U	C	P	I	C	P	T	Q	R
W	E	K	I	N	G	D	O	M	I	R	E	X	E	I
N	N	T	X	G	Z	Y	U	B	M	R	D	M	D	C
R	X	O	R	O	L	I	N	Q	M	B	I	T	X	X
Q	M	K	M	O	D	E	S	P	I	S	E	T	H	G
X	M	M	H	D	F	L	E	S	S	S	N	V	V	V
A	N	E	N	N	K	M	L	I	Y	C	T	K	P	W
O	M	M	D	E	R	U	O	P	U	T	P	S	Y	T
D	P	V	I	S	S	N	R	C	S	B	X	R	N	N
V	B	R	C	S	Q	I	G	G	X	C	K	Z	B	Z
Y	E	C	N	T	J	A	Q	R	F	Q	L	M	J	U
F	G	W	J	I	A	J	T	G	J	P	A	Q	C	U
U	S	Y	Q	X	X	Z	A	T	T	E	H	U	G	X

~~~~ *HONOR* ~~~~

To honor is to have respect, reverence, and high esteem for someone who has positively impacted your life or the lives of others by their actions. We bestow honor upon people who serve the Lord. Christians give honor to God through praise and worship - glorifying His name because He is the Savior and there is no one greater than the Lord.

(Read & find the bold and underlined words)

A man's pride shall bring him low: but **honour** shall uphold the humble in spirit. *Proverbs 29:23 (KJV)*

19 Do you not know that your body is a **temple** of the Holy Spirit,
who is in you, whom you have received from God? You are not
your own; 20 you were bought at a **price**. Therefore honor God
with your body. *1 Corinthians 6:19-20 (NIV)*

My salvation and my honor depend on God; he is my mighty **rock**, my **refuge**. *Psalm 62:7 (NIV)*

He who **oppresses** the poor shows **contempt** for their **Maker**, but whoever is kind to the needy honors God. *Proverbs 14:31 (NIV)*

He who speaks on his own does so to **gain** honor for himself, but he who works for the honor of the one who sent him is a man of truth; there is nothing false about him. *John 7:18 (NIV)*

And if one member suffers, all the members suffer with it; or if one member is **honored**, all the **members** rejoice with it. *1 Corinthians 12:26 (NKJV)*

9 Honor the Lord with your **substance** and with the first fruits of
all your produce; 10 then your barns will be filled with **plenty**, and
your vats will be **bursting** with wine. *Proverbs 3:9-10 (NRSV)*

HONOR

E	J	L	K	N	S	D	N	S	K	D	Z	X	P	T
S	F	R	E	F	U	G	E	W	N	L	Y	L	P	H
H	S	X	Z	I	B	S	O	R	A	R	E	X	I	K
K	Z	F	B	V	S	C	R	U	O	N	O	H	D	F
Q	O	M	U	E	T	P	M	E	T	N	O	C	Z	N
I	V	Q	R	C	A	O	J	Y	B	D	O	B	K	H
E	Q	P	S	I	N	I	A	G	A	M	W	H	J	I
T	P	K	T	R	C	O	D	S	H	K	E	O	P	P
O	D	E	I	P	E	Q	D	G	J	L	A	M	O	A
M	P	D	N	L	D	K	P	C	P	E	R	X	R	E
P	V	L	G	H	M	V	A	M	M	F	O	N	E	H
J	O	G	Z	S	V	V	E	M	I	J	Q	Z	M	E
U	R	J	I	A	J	T	N	X	E	W	H	N	R	Q
V	S	L	X	W	H	R	P	J	N	Q	K	Q	I	E
B	Q	U	K	A	B	D	J	O	Y	Q	D	B	U	U

~~~~ *HOPE* ~~~~

When there is hope in the Lord, our destiny is much brighter. Believing in God keeps us hopeful for the best that life has to offer. The Book of Isaiah reminds us that if we wait on the Lord, our strength will be renewed. Expect positive outcomes in your life, and give thanks to God for fulfilling His promises.

(Read & find the bold and underlined words)

23 O love the LORD, all ye his saints: for the LORD **<u>preserveth</u>**
the faithful, and plentifully **<u>rewardeth</u>** the **<u>proud</u>** doer. 24 Be of
good courage, and he shall strengthen your heart, all ye that hope
in the LORD. *Psalm 31:23-24 (KJV)*

13 May my accusers **<u>perish</u>** in shame; may those who want to harm
me be **<u>covered</u>** with scorn and disgrace. 14 But as for me, I will
always have hope; I will praise you more and more. 15 My mouth
will tell of your righteousness, of your salvation all day long,
though I know not its **<u>measure</u>**. *Psalm 71:13-15 (NIV)*

May the God of hope fill you with all joy and peace as you **<u>trust</u>** in him, so that you may **<u>overflow</u>** with hope by the power of the Holy Spirit. *Romans 15:13 (NIV)*

The hope of the righteous will be gladness, But the **<u>expectation</u>** of the wicked will perish. *Proverbs 10:28 (NKJV)*

Now **<u>hope</u>** does not disappoint, because the love of God has been poured out in our hearts by the Holy Spirit who was given to us. *Romans 5:5 (NKJV)*

Let us hold fast the **<u>confession</u>** of our hope without wavering, for He who promised is faithful. *Hebrews 10:23 (NKJV)*

24 For in hope we were saved. Now hope that is seen is not hope.
For who hopes for what is seen? 25 But if we hope for what we do
not see, we wait for it with **<u>patience</u>**. *Romans 8:24-25 (NRSV)*

HOPE

E	X	P	E	C	T	A	T	I	O	N	T	U	I	D
H	O	P	E	H	M	Q	I	R	V	O	Y	R	E	E
T	T	P	O	W	T	Y	O	E	U	I	J	M	G	J
J	I	E	F	W	Q	V	Z	P	H	S	D	H	I	T
F	X	A	D	L	E	G	S	L	K	S	T	D	E	X
M	Y	H	F	R	C	I	E	C	N	E	I	T	A	P
C	W	V	F	U	A	K	J	D	V	F	H	R	O	P
C	U	L	Q	Y	L	W	Y	R	U	N	O	T	E	V
V	O	V	W	F	W	O	E	H	Y	O	R	Y	K	P
W	F	V	E	C	X	S	L	R	U	C	R	E	X	S
T	T	F	E	N	E	O	T	K	U	Q	S	P	N	O
B	T	R	B	R	K	B	D	T	L	S	W	U	J	J
M	F	E	P	L	E	Q	B	U	E	W	A	H	J	O
N	D	W	Y	L	S	D	L	L	I	N	F	E	F	H
A	V	X	V	R	S	U	O	Q	R	Z	M	P	M	O

~~~~ *HUMBLE* ~~~~

Humility is a very special virtue. A person can be honest or confident about their unique abilities, yet modest enough to display a thankful spirit. Boasting with pride will not gain much respect, but an unassuming disposition can gain the hearts of many.

(Read & find the bold and underlined words)

Take my yoke upon you and learn from me, for I am **gentle** and **humble** in heart, and you will find **rest** for your souls. *Matthew 11:29 (NIV)*

8 **Good** and upright is the LORD; Therefore He teaches sinners in
the way. 9 The humble He **guides** in justice, And the humble He
teaches His way. *Psalm 25:8-9 (NKJV)*

33 The curse of the LORD is on the house of the wicked, But He
blesses the home of the just. 34 Surely He scorns the **scornful**, But
gives grace to the humble. *Proverbs 3:33-34 (NKJV)*

Therefore whoever humbles himself as this **little** child is the **greatest** in the kingdom of heaven. *Matthew 18:4 (NKJV)*

5 Likewise you younger people, **submit** yourselves to your **elders**.
Yes, all of you be **submissive** to one another, and be clothed with
humility, for "God resists the proud, But gives grace to the
humble." 6 Therefore humble yourselves under the mighty hand of
God, that He may exalt you in due time, 7 casting all your care
upon Him, for He cares for you. *1 Peter 5:5-7 (NKJV)*

Humble **yourselves** before the Lord, and he will exalt you. *James 4:10 (NRSV)*

HUMBLE

X	M	Y	I	T	I	M	B	U	S	H	H	P	U	S
I	G	Y	S	Q	Y	P	M	U	W	D	W	W	L	R
H	O	E	M	X	G	C	B	C	Q	K	S	V	H	E
V	R	U	V	H	U	M	B	L	E	I	Q	N	M	B
T	N	J	M	I	I	N	L	U	L	W	V	Y	L	Q
S	J	Z	C	S	D	S	Z	U	T	Y	W	J	L	F
E	A	B	S	C	E	G	E	N	T	L	E	F	M	J
T	A	I	P	O	S	V	G	I	I	F	G	S	S	N
A	V	J	S	R	E	D	L	E	L	N	M	N	P	S
E	P	Q	D	N	A	I	O	E	V	W	T	A	O	W
R	T	N	F	F	M	F	Z	O	S	R	R	T	K	E
G	B	Y	R	U	J	V	U	V	G	R	B	S	K	Q
I	D	P	H	L	M	O	F	X	Z	Q	U	C	E	J
S	S	C	J	T	J	U	O	W	L	K	X	O	I	V
S	Z	O	G	Z	U	K	Q	S	A	C	R	Y	Y	E

~~~~ *INSPIRATION* ~~~~

Have you ever been inspired by a dynamic motivational speaker, a few words of encouragement, a self-improvement seminar, or someone who overcame seemingly impossible challenges? The feeling is stimulating, and it creates an internal desire to excel. Teachers inspire their students, and parents inspire their children. The Bible was inspired by God and each Book reveals divine guidance for Christians who seek eternal life through Jesus Christ.

(Read & find the bold and underlined words)

But there is a spirit in man: and the **inspiration** of the Almighty giveth them **understanding**. *Job 32:8 (KJV)*

2 We **always** thank God for all of you, **mentioning** you in our
prayers. 3 We **continually** remember before our God and Father
your work produced by faith, your labor **prompted** by love, and
your endurance inspired by hope in our Lord Jesus Christ.
1 Thessalonians 1:2-3 (NIV)

16 All scripture is **inspired** by God and is useful for teaching, for
reproof, for **correction**, and for training in righteousness, 17 so
that everyone who belongs to God may be **proficient**, equipped for
every good work. *2 Timothy 3:16-17 (NRSV)*

Anxiety in the heart of man causes **depression**, But a good **word** makes it glad. *Proverbs 12:25 (NKJV)*

INSPIRATION

U	N	D	E	R	S	T	A	N	D	I	N	G	Y	B
Y	P	O	G	W	I	D	U	O	K	N	H	I	S	W
D	L	Z	I	N	Y	L	E	I	M	S	O	G	T	I
E	V	L	A	S	I	V	W	T	B	P	J	S	W	D
T	W	D	A	L	S	N	P	A	D	I	P	X	Z	Y
P	O	S	L	U	W	E	O	R	A	R	T	H	O	X
M	T	D	S	G	N	A	R	I	Z	E	V	X	D	W
O	H	M	K	B	G	I	Y	P	T	D	G	T	P	P
R	W	F	G	C	G	E	T	S	E	N	E	H	U	G
P	R	O	F	I	C	I	E	N	T	D	E	L	F	P
L	C	O	R	R	E	C	T	I	O	N	P	M	V	L
J	O	R	V	D	N	J	V	W	P	C	N	G	M	W
F	W	P	D	U	C	C	L	Z	O	M	S	O	U	I
Y	K	E	X	Z	E	N	B	I	R	Q	D	T	R	O
X	W	R	C	K	G	V	D	M	H	F	A	B	Z	C

~~~~ *INTEGRITY* ~~~~

Establishing an honest personal code of ethics or morals will be revealed in your character – on your job and in all of your relationships. People determine whether or not you are trustworthy based on your commitment. Live with integrity – walk your talk!

(Read & find the bold and underlined words)

Joyful are people of integrity, who follow the **instructions** of the LORD. *Psalm 119:1 (NLT)*

The LORD judges the peoples; judge me, O LORD, according to my righteousness and according to the **integrity** that is in me. *Psalm 7:8 (NRSV)*

Vindicate me, O LORD, For I have walked in my integrity. I have also trusted in the LORD; I shall not slip. *Psalm 26:1 (NKJV)*

6 **Likewise**, exhort the young men to be **sober-minded**, 7 in all
things showing yourself to be a pattern of good works; in doctrine
showing integrity, **reverence**, incorruptibility, 8 sound **speech** that
cannot be condemned, that one who is an opponent may be
ashamed, having nothing evil to say of you. *Titus 2:6-8 (NKJV)*

So in everything, do to **others** what you would have them do to you, for this **sums** up the Law and the Prophets. *Matthew 7:12 (NIV)*

So I **strive** always to keep my **conscience** clear before God and man. *Acts 24:16 (NIV)*

INTEGRITY

I	T	C	L	X	M	E	J	E	S	F	N	P	W	K
I	N	J	H	E	S	I	W	E	K	I	L	L	Q	B
G	J	S	V	V	T	J	S	U	M	S	S	Z	V	U
J	L	N	T	I	Y	A	W	H	P	Q	G	I	V	B
R	E	V	E	R	E	N	C	E	Y	U	K	D	Y	J
V	H	P	T	T	U	X	E	I	S	R	E	H	T	O
A	K	I	X	S	Q	C	M	Y	D	D	K	A	W	H
I	W	H	K	B	H	L	T	T	N	N	I	H	L	P
R	B	Z	C	I	P	C	Z	I	J	U	I	F	U	B
M	M	W	I	F	I	T	M	R	O	N	O	V	F	T
F	F	Q	G	F	J	R	D	G	A	N	P	F	Y	B
U	W	V	T	I	E	C	N	E	I	C	S	N	O	C
R	B	M	Z	B	O	O	R	T	X	L	V	X	J	P
B	E	I	O	D	J	E	O	N	H	S	I	W	H	U
W	W	S	U	I	I	F	R	I	W	C	M	G	K	G

~~~~ *JOY* ~~~~

The feeling of joy comes straight from the heart. If there is joy in your environment, then there will be joy in your heart. We often rejoice over the great accomplishments of family members or our favorite sports team. Reflect on the greatness of the Lord, and rejoice because He is worthy of all praise. Trouble and heartache may pay an unexpected visit, but the Epistle of James reminds us to "…count it all joy."

(Read & find the bold and underlined words)

"**Behold**, this is the **joy** of His way, And out of the earth others will grow. *Job 8:19 (NKJV)*

I have told you this so that my joy may be in you and that your joy may be **complete**. *John 15:11 (NIV)*

But let all who take refuge in you **rejoice**; let them sing joyful **praises** forever. Spread your protection over them, that all who love your name may be filled with joy. *Psalm 5:11 (NLT)*

The commandments of the Lord are right, bringing joy to the heart. The commands of the Lord are clear, giving **insight** for living. *Psalm 19:8 (NLT)*

I take joy in **doing** your will, my God, for your instructions are written on my heart." *Psalm 40:8 (NLT)*

May all who fear you find in me a **cause** for joy, for I have put my hope in your word. *Psalm 119:74 (NLT)*

16 After his **baptism**, as Jesus came up out of the water, the
heavens were opened and he saw the Spirit of God **descending** like
a dove and **settling** on him. 17 And a **voice** from heaven said, "This
is my **dearly** loved Son, who brings me great joy."
Matthew 3:16-17 (NLT)

JOY

C	L	Z	N	M	D	O	I	N	G	I	M	X	L	A
O	E	Y	O	C	H	X	K	N	R	O	Q	E	A	C
C	G	L	L	A	F	V	I	H	S	G	S	W	O	X
E	N	R	O	U	V	D	O	B	F	I	W	Q	B	M
V	I	A	T	S	N	A	A	I	G	K	G	N	V	V
G	L	E	T	E	L	P	M	O	C	M	U	H	A	V
D	T	D	C	S	T	D	L	C	B	E	H	F	T	D
D	T	S	O	I	J	N	Q	J	Z	B	F	W	L	C
Y	E	J	S	A	O	T	A	M	N	I	Z	B	P	D
D	S	M	X	R	Y	J	O	F	K	N	E	M	P	G
B	L	Y	A	P	D	S	E	F	Z	E	G	J	M	P
A	W	O	Q	D	A	G	O	R	K	L	Y	F	L	U
W	I	N	H	X	Y	A	X	M	E	Z	M	I	P	N
T	M	R	O	E	Q	M	C	G	X	Y	J	E	Y	D
B	H	L	R	G	B	S	Z	H	C	F	U	T	S	C

~~~~ *KNOWLEDGE* ~~~~

Whether we take a class or seek information from another person – we are growing in knowledge – increasing our level of intelligence. To be informed leads the way to better decision-making. God is omniscient, and if we are Christ-like, our knowledge will turn into wisdom.

(Read & find the bold and underlined words)

Now give me wisdom and **knowledge**, that I may go out and come in before this people; for who can judge this great people of Yours?" *2 Chronicles 1:10 (NKJV)*

A truly wise **person** uses few words; a person with understanding is **even-tempered**. *Proverbs 17:27 (NLT)*

Talk no more so exceeding proudly; let not **arrogancy** come out of your mouth: for the LORD is a God of knowledge, and by him actions are **weighed**. *1 Samuel 2:3 (KJV)*

The fear of the LORD is the **beginning** of knowledge: but fools despise wisdom and instruction. *Proverbs 1:7 (KJV)*

And the LORD God made all kinds of **trees** grow out of the ground—trees that were pleasing to the eye and good for food. In the middle of the **garden** were the tree of life and the tree of the knowledge of good and evil. *Genesis 2:9 (NIV)*

5 For this very reason, make every **effort** to add to your faith
goodness; and to goodness, knowledge; 6 and to knowledge, self-
control; and to **self-control**, perseverance; and to perseverance,
godliness; 7 and to godliness, brotherly kindness; and to **brotherly**
kindness, love. 8 For if you possess these qualities in increasing
measure, they will keep you from being **ineffective** and **unproductive** in your knowledge of our Lord Jesus Christ. *2 Peter 1:5-8 (NIV)*

KNOWLEDGE

D	E	R	E	P	M	E	T	N	E	V	E	B	O	A
A	N	V	V	U	I	V	Z	F	V	W	G	E	Z	F
B	E	G	I	N	N	I	N	G	S	E	D	H	O	B
S	W	X	T	T	Y	T	R	O	F	F	E	X	G	Y
A	E	Z	C	Z	C	Y	J	E	W	N	L	P	T	S
D	I	L	E	S	N	U	T	B	K	O	W	U	B	K
D	G	E	F	F	A	F	D	R	E	S	O	D	F	K
V	H	N	F	C	G	I	F	O	E	R	N	L	I	R
F	E	B	E	O	O	Q	D	T	R	E	K	V	P	V
F	D	O	N	D	R	N	G	H	C	P	S	E	P	Y
B	E	I	I	V	R	Q	T	E	X	G	N	Q	V	I
P	Y	G	V	B	A	A	X	R	Q	H	P	U	I	O
F	P	T	I	C	R	D	G	L	O	F	G	O	E	D
F	N	C	E	P	C	T	C	Y	X	L	E	K	P	G
C	J	I	Y	P	I	G	L	L	H	M	R	W	Z	E

~~~~ *LEADERS* ~~~~

The Book of Hebrews describes Jesus as a perfect leader. The role of a servant leader is admirable to God because you are working for Him. To lead someone or a group of people is also to serve them. The ability to influence others is a powerful position. Remember that your reputation and style of leadership will determine your success.

(Read & find the bold and underlined words)

<u>Choose</u> some well-respected men from each **<u>tribe</u>** who are known for their wisdom and understanding, and I will appoint them as your leaders.' *Deuteronomy 1:13 (NLT)*

Without wise leadership, a nation falls; there is **<u>safety</u>** in having many **<u>advisers</u>**. *Proverbs 11:14 (NLT)*

When there is **<u>moral</u>** rot within a nation, its government **<u>topples</u>** easily. But wise and **<u>knowledgeable</u>** leaders bring **<u>stability</u>**. *Proverbs 28:2 (NLT)*

25 Jesus told them, "In this world the kings and great men lord it
over their people, yet they are called 'friends of the people.' 26 But
among you it will be different. Those who are the greatest among
you should take the lowest **<u>rank</u>**, and the leader should be like a
<u>servant</u>. 27 Who is more **<u>important</u>**, the one who sits at the table
or the one who serves? The one who sits at the table, of course. But
not here! For I am among you as one who serves.
Luke 22:25-27 (NLT)

Do your best to present yourself to God as one **<u>approved</u>** by him, a worker who has no need to be ashamed, rightly **<u>explaining</u>** the word of truth. *2 Timothy 2:15 (NRSV)*

LEADERS

G	N	I	N	I	A	L	P	X	E	T	O	N	V	N
E	F	J	M	O	L	P	G	P	N	Y	V	O	Z	M
C	X	Y	A	P	H	G	D	A	W	T	N	U	K	H
N	K	D	P	D	O	T	V	B	K	I	M	Z	N	Q
V	N	C	P	U	V	R	V	S	E	L	P	P	O	T
S	N	S	R	L	E	I	T	R	U	I	K	P	W	Z
C	H	O	O	S	E	B	S	A	R	B	L	Z	L	E
E	P	J	V	G	A	E	W	E	N	A	I	Z	E	S
X	E	T	E	U	Z	F	J	Q	R	T	N	T	D	E
A	E	A	D	U	E	Z	E	O	L	S	F	K	G	P
Q	U	L	Z	Q	O	P	M	T	R	N	C	A	E	P
G	N	H	X	G	T	F	X	I	Y	V	Q	V	A	W
I	B	W	V	J	J	G	Y	T	U	Q	B	Z	B	W
S	I	M	X	C	N	E	D	O	B	Z	X	S	L	T
C	G	D	J	M	L	T	J	F	N	I	M	W	E	K

~~~~ *LIFE* ~~~~

Energy is life, and life is a gift from God. How much time do you spend on personal development? The more we invest in ourselves, the more equipped we become to make contributions to the world. Your environment and the choices you make shape your life. If you don't like your environment, change it. There is truth in the statement that advises, "If you want something different, you have to do something different." Engage in self-discovery. Get the best out of life and remember that the blood of Jesus prevails over any gloomy situation.

(Read & find the bold and underlined words)

And the LORD God **formed** man of the **dust** of the ground, and **breathed** into his **nostrils** the breath of life; and man became a living soul. *Genesis 2:7 (KJV)*

Surely goodness and mercy shall follow me all the days of my **life**: and I will dwell in the house of the LORD for ever. *Psalm 23:6 (KJV)*

Turn my **eyes** away from worthless things; **preserve** my life according to your word. *Psalm 119:37 (NIV)*

Doesn't your reverence for God give you **confidence**? Doesn't your life of integrity give you hope? *Job 4:6 (NLT)*

Teach us to **realize** the **brevity** of life, so that we may grow in wisdom. *Psalm 90:12 (NLT)*

And this is the message I proclaim—that the day is coming when God, through Christ Jesus, will judge everyone's **secret** life. *Romans 2:16 (NLT)*

When Christ who is your life is **revealed**, then you also will be revealed with him in glory. *Colossians 3:4 (NRSV)*

LIFE

B	N	E	F	I	L	Y	P	Q	S	L	P	F	P	J
R	O	V	U	G	J	Q	T	O	F	W	K	P	C	S
E	S	R	Y	R	Z	E	Q	F	F	Z	V	C	P	I
A	T	E	B	F	X	D	M	D	M	O	E	A	U	K
T	R	S	C	O	N	F	I	D	E	N	C	E	N	H
H	I	E	K	R	Q	I	W	Q	O	N	P	M	W	K
E	L	R	V	M	E	O	X	C	R	C	Y	W	D	S
D	S	P	C	E	M	T	S	E	Y	E	S	T	E	T
G	V	B	I	D	A	K	A	H	W	S	R	C	K	B
R	E	S	S	U	W	L	X	X	R	V	P	C	O	M
G	D	X	Y	T	I	V	E	R	B	K	E	H	D	F
O	Q	E	R	Z	V	H	O	D	V	K	T	L	L	M
C	N	I	E	V	V	C	G	R	U	V	D	Y	H	K
R	H	N	S	U	L	Q	M	N	O	S	A	V	D	Y
M	J	J	R	Y	T	C	W	C	J	I	T	N	H	Z

~~~~ *LIGHT* ~~~~

Remember that Jesus is the light of the world. If you encounter misfortune, immediately search for the light of the matter. When family and friends are in need, be the sunshine in the midst of their darkness. Oftentimes, it may take no more than a genuine smile.

(Read & find the bold and underlined words)

Let your light so **shine** before men, that they may see your good works and glorify your Father in heaven. *Matthew 5:16 (NKJV)*

Blessed is the people that know the joyful **sound**: they shall walk, O LORD, in the **light** of thy countenance. *Psalm 89:15 (KJV)*

Rejoice not against me, O mine enemy: when I fall, I shall arise; when I sit in **darkness**, the LORD shall be a light unto me. *Micah 7:8 (KJV)*

Then **spake** Jesus again unto them, saying, I am the light of the world: he that **followeth** me shall not walk in darkness, but shall have the light of life. *John 8:12 (KJV)*

18 The path of the righteous is like the first **gleam** of dawn, shining
ever **brighter** till the full light of day. 19 But the way of the wicked
is like deep darkness; they do not know what makes them
stumble. 20 My son, pay **attention** to what I say; listen closely to
my words. *Proverbs 4:18-20 (NIV)*

For everything that is **hidden** will eventually be brought into the open, and every secret will be brought to light. *Mark 4:22 (NLT)*

6 If we say that we have fellowship with him while we are **walking**
in darkness, we lie and do not do what is true; 7 but if we walk in
the light as he himself is in the light, we have fellowship with one
another, and the blood of Jesus his Son **cleanses** us from all sin.
1 John 1:6-7 (NRSV)

LIGHT

C	R	L	H	I	F	C	H	A	E	E	Q	G	W	E
V	L	R	L	I	G	H	T	E	W	O	L	L	O	F
O	Y	E	H	K	O	T	S	J	A	E	I	A	B	B
K	W	T	A	H	E	S	P	M	A	A	V	K	B	F
G	S	H	I	N	E	L	B	M	U	T	S	E	A	D
S	N	G	T	N	S	Y	X	Z	T	S	Z	R	U	V
O	V	I	K	Z	N	E	D	D	I	H	Z	M	R	K
U	O	R	K	O	A	I	S	I	M	F	E	H	J	H
N	A	B	O	L	N	P	P	W	R	W	N	K	V	B
D	A	H	F	H	A	L	P	N	K	Q	C	P	R	C
E	M	I	C	K	O	W	M	F	B	Y	P	G	F	G
B	P	U	E	F	R	R	B	K	V	M	F	G	U	N
D	O	R	Z	P	I	T	S	Z	X	L	B	Z	G	A
R	Z	I	R	J	J	W	V	G	U	R	O	R	X	K
R	Y	L	Z	O	W	T	C	G	D	O	X	Z	L	Y

~~~~ *LIVE* ~~~~

It is pleasing to God when believers live according to His will. If you don't know what His will is for your life, you'll have to search your heart, and listen to the Holy Spirit. There is a verse from a song that reminds us that because God lives "*I can face tomorrow.*" Living in today's world can break your spirit, but if you serve the Almighty – you are alive in Christ Jesus. Life becomes worth living when you know that God is the navigator of your future.

(Read & find the bold and underlined words)

If we **live** in the Spirit, let us also walk in the Spirit. *Galatians 5:25 (KJV)*

For in him we live, and move, and have our being; as **certain** also of your own **poets** have said, For we are also his **offspring**. *Acts 17:28 (KJV)*

18 I will not leave you as **orphans**; I will come to you. 19 Before
long, the **world** will not see me anymore, but you will see me.
Because I live, you also will live. 20 On that day you will realize
that I am in my Father, and you are in me, and I am in you.
John 14:18-20 (NIV)

76 May your **unfailing** love be my comfort, according to your
promise to your servant. 77 Let your compassion come to me that I
may live, for your law is my delight. *Psalm 119:76-77 (NIV)*

Sin is no **longer** your master, for you no longer live under the **requirements** of the law. Instead, you live under the **freedom** of God's grace. *Romans 6:14 (NLT)*

Those who live in the **shelter** of the Most High will find rest in the **shadow** of the Almighty. *Psalm 91:1 (NLT)*

LIVE

S	O	P	O	D	O	C	G	G	X	I	L	N	K	T
T	T	F	P	O	E	T	S	N	A	H	P	R	O	B
N	D	R	F	R	K	S	Q	I	C	O	G	T	T	F
E	A	E	L	S	H	I	S	L	N	A	F	N	I	L
M	A	E	A	A	P	H	A	I	O	T	D	B	Z	M
E	A	D	D	C	E	R	T	A	I	N	S	A	K	L
R	A	O	O	L	V	A	I	F	I	B	G	F	X	W
I	W	M	T	K	I	U	E	N	R	M	J	E	B	V
U	O	E	I	E	L	A	W	U	G	A	F	N	R	U
Q	R	G	N	T	E	B	I	U	T	S	Z	P	Y	F
E	L	S	H	G	Y	J	X	U	I	G	O	K	Q	P
R	D	L	X	J	U	I	M	R	S	P	N	P	L	X
T	X	Z	L	H	Q	G	K	P	H	O	N	E	P	C
I	W	O	E	W	H	M	U	R	W	L	K	S	Q	H
W	W	B	S	B	X	O	Q	G	W	W	J	Y	S	A

~~~~ *LORD* ~~~~

Christians acknowledge Jesus Christ as their Lord and Savior. He is the Way – possessing full power and dominion. It is important that we establish a deep relationship with Him. Jesus is the way to eternal life.

(Read & find the bold and underlined words)

Blessed is the nation whose God is the **LORD**; and the people whom he hath chosen for his own **inheritance**. *Psalm 33:12 (KJV)*

And therefore will the LORD wait, that he may be **gracious** unto you, and therefore will he be exalted, that he may have mercy upon you: for the LORD is a God of **judgment**: blessed are all they that wait for him. *Isaiah 30:18 (KJV)*

For the eyes of the LORD run to and fro throughout the whole earth, to show Himself strong on **behalf** of those whose heart is **loyal** to Him. *2 Chronicles 16:9 (NKJV)*

“You are worthy, O Lord, To receive glory and honor and **power**; For You created all things, And by Your will they exist and were created.” *Revelation 4:11 (NKJV)*

9 Therefore God also has highly exalted Him and given Him the
name which is above every **name**, 10 that at the name of Jesus
every knee should bow, of those in heaven, and of those on earth,
and of those under the earth, 11 and that every **tongue** should
confess that Jesus **Christ** is Lord, to the glory of God the Father.
Philippians 2:9-11 (NKJV)

18 Truly the eye of the LORD is on those who fear him, on those
who hope in his **steadfast** love, 19 to deliver their soul from death,
and to keep them alive in **famine**. 20 Our soul waits for the LORD;
he is our help and shield. *Psalm 33:18-20 (NRSV)*

LORD

D	U	E	V	C	S	O	Q	B	Y	I	Y	Q	E	I
V	M	I	J	U	D	G	M	E	N	T	W	N	D	Q
K	E	X	T	A	S	V	H	H	O	J	I	O	T	W
L	I	M	S	H	U	H	E	A	D	M	W	T	S	V
B	T	F	A	L	O	R	D	L	A	J	G	X	K	G
H	I	J	F	N	I	K	O	F	P	B	Y	Z	N	A
Y	E	D	D	T	C	Y	C	T	P	S	R	M	T	M
P	T	I	A	H	A	H	O	L	S	F	V	K	G	A
O	R	N	E	L	R	N	G	E	X	F	G	B	M	W
W	C	D	T	I	G	S	N	S	L	F	T	L	Y	B
E	N	U	S	U	N	G	U	V	A	U	Q	H	C	H
R	V	T	E	Y	H	E	V	C	F	O	T	B	A	S
A	J	L	C	Q	C	D	N	I	S	I	S	B	H	Z
R	U	D	O	K	Z	X	V	A	W	A	T	D	B	O
Q	D	E	L	M	S	P	Q	X	B	E	T	K	B	C

~~~~ *LOVE* ~~~~

The ability to love requires sincere action and commitment. You give love and receive love in various ways. It keeps you positively connected to an individual, family member, neighbor, or friend. A person can also love their job or mission – which means that they have passion for their work based upon fulfilling certain outcomes. It is better to love than to hate. God is love!

(Read & find the bold and underlined words)

12 My command is this: **Love** each other as I have loved you. 13
Greater love has no one than this, that he lay down his life for his
friends. *John 15:12-13 (NIV)*

9 Love must be **sincere**. Hate what is evil; cling to what is good.
10 Be **devoted** to one another in brotherly love. Honor one another
above yourselves. *Romans 12:9-10 (NIV)*

1 **Imitate** God, therefore, in everything you do, because you are his
dear children. 2 Live a life filled with love, following the **example**
of Christ. He loved us and offered himself as a sacrifice for us, a
pleasing **aroma** to God. *Ephesians 5:1-2 (NLT)*

You shall not take **vengeance**, nor bear any **grudge** against the children of your people, but you shall love your **neighbor** as yourself: I am the LORD. *Leviticus 19:18 (NKJV)*

And now **abide** faith, hope, love, these three; but the greatest of these is love. *1 Corinthians 13:13 (NKJV)*

Pursue love and strive for the spiritual gifts, and especially that you may **prophesy**. *1 Corinthians 14:1 (NRSV)*

LOVE

B	W	J	E	S	C	Y	S	E	H	P	O	R	P	X
S	H	A	W	Y	A	M	C	V	T	Q	D	P	Z	E
B	Z	M	N	B	Q	N	P	O	L	A	Q	C	V	R
J	P	O	E	X	A	M	P	L	E	M	T	B	P	E
R	F	R	I	E	N	D	S	U	U	L	Y	I	I	C
D	H	A	G	Z	X	T	U	F	S	G	L	K	M	N
V	E	N	H	H	C	R	Z	K	R	K	M	K	V	I
U	E	V	B	D	F	G	R	U	U	Z	A	K	R	S
V	G	J	O	E	Y	E	D	E	P	D	R	B	B	B
A	O	L	R	T	L	G	U	D	K	I	T	C	A	R
Y	A	Z	M	D	E	T	W	A	L	F	I	F	U	W
C	K	I	O	U	E	D	P	S	J	Q	O	K	L	H
Z	B	E	C	Y	F	N	I	K	B	X	V	G	A	Q
B	T	M	C	G	N	M	M	B	Y	B	K	D	T	S
V	T	D	V	U	C	F	B	K	A	U	H	N	Z	L

~~~~ *MARRIAGE* ~~~~

Marriage is more than a legal document or a beautiful ceremony. It is a sacred commitment and an intimate association between a husband and wife who have professed their eternal love for one another. The challenges of life can destroy a marriage, but God is able conquer those challenges for partners who place Him first in their lives.

(Read & find the bold and underlined words)

2 Nevertheless, to avoid **<u>fornication</u>**, let every man have his own
<u>wife</u>, and let every woman have her own husband. 3 Let the
<u>husband</u> render unto the wife due **<u>benevolence</u>**: and likewise also
the wife unto the husband. *1 Corinthians 7:2-3 (KJV)*

4 Give honor to marriage, and **<u>remain</u>** faithful to one another in
<u>marriage</u>. God will surely judge people who are immoral and
those who **<u>commit</u>** adultery. 5 Don't love money; be **<u>satisfied</u>** with
what you have. For God has said, "I will never fail you. I will
never abandon you." *Hebrews 13:4-5 (NLT)*

9 Two are **<u>better</u>** than one, Because they have a good reward for
their labor. 10 For if they fall, one will **<u>lift</u>** up his **<u>companion</u>**. But
woe to him who is alone when he falls, For he has no one to help
him up. 11 Again, if two lie down together, they will keep **<u>warm</u>**;
But how can one be warm alone? *Ecclesiastes 4:9-11 (NKJV)*

4 And He answered and said to them, "Have you not read that He
who made them at the beginning 'made them male and female,' 5
and said, 'For this reason a man shall leave his father and mother
and be **<u>joined</u>** to his wife, and the two shall become one flesh'?
6 So then, they are no longer two but one flesh. Therefore what
God has joined **<u>together</u>**, let not man separate."
Matthew 19:4-6 (NKJV)

MARRIAGE

F	O	R	N	I	C	A	T	I	O	N	B	N	G	Y
R	L	D	L	O	W	L	K	B	C	P	Z	R	E	M
D	E	I	F	S	I	T	A	S	N	V	A	O	C	Y
N	G	H	M	F	F	N	I	F	Y	P	Y	C	N	D
A	A	D	T	R	E	M	A	I	N	K	O	W	E	G
B	I	B	N	E	A	J	O	P	G	M	U	N	L	T
S	R	Q	B	T	G	W	L	A	M	O	I	P	O	X
U	R	B	R	T	T	O	Y	I	S	O	X	V	V	A
H	A	T	P	E	Y	W	T	D	J	R	C	B	E	X
C	M	O	I	B	T	P	C	W	X	Y	P	P	N	H
E	Y	V	R	Y	M	P	O	M	O	C	H	N	E	V
E	X	K	K	S	A	T	D	Z	X	N	D	P	B	S
Z	A	Z	P	J	H	S	Q	D	I	O	P	R	S	M
V	H	N	C	J	B	C	R	K	I	X	L	K	Z	M
N	U	E	D	D	R	B	G	B	B	I	Q	Q	D	R

~~~~ *MERCY* ~~~~

During the dark moments of our life, we often shout, "Lord, please have mercy." The good news is that God displays divine favor everyday – even though we may have to suffer the consequences of our actions. Just as we are blessed, we are to be a blessing and show mercy toward others.

(Read & find the bold and underlined words)

Let us therefore come **<u>boldly</u>** unto the throne of grace, that we may obtain mercy, and find grace to help in time of need. *Hebrews 4:16 (KJV)*

<u>Surely</u> goodness and **<u>mercy</u>** shall follow me all the days of my life: and I will dwell in the house of the LORD for ever. *Psalm 23:6 (KJV)*

Who is a God like you, who **<u>pardons</u>** sin and forgives the **<u>transgression</u>** of the **<u>remnant</u>** of his inheritance? You do not stay angry forever but **<u>delight</u>** to show mercy. *Micah 7:18 (NIV)*

When all the children of **<u>Israel</u>** saw how the fire came down, and the glory of the LORD on the temple, they bowed their faces to the ground on the **<u>pavement</u>**, and worshiped and praised the LORD, saying: "For He is good, For His mercy **<u>endures</u>** forever." *2Chronicles 7:3 (NKJV)*

12 So speak and so act as those who are to be judged by the law of
<u>liberty</u>. 13 For judgment will be without mercy to anyone who has shown no mercy; mercy **<u>triumphs</u>** over judgment. *James 2:12-13 (NRSV)*

MERCY

T	R	A	N	S	G	R	E	S	S	I	O	N	G	X
P	N	G	T	L	B	S	P	H	U	X	Z	Z	E	D
U	S	E	R	U	D	N	E	P	R	Y	C	R	E	M
J	M	M	M	D	A	O	J	M	E	M	L	L	D	B
F	A	I	K	E	R	D	R	U	L	R	I	U	L	Q
G	E	X	S	F	V	R	W	I	Y	G	B	X	L	F
R	V	Q	H	R	E	A	D	R	H	O	E	I	A	R
U	E	Q	Q	M	A	P	P	T	L	Q	R	T	I	T
B	S	N	N	V	G	E	V	D	V	A	T	T	A	O
E	O	A	X	R	D	Z	L	Q	U	V	Y	V	U	X
N	N	K	X	D	F	Y	F	E	V	A	U	P	L	W
T	M	Y	M	H	R	J	X	M	P	H	F	C	A	Z
C	J	T	N	A	G	A	N	M	B	Q	Y	M	R	U
A	U	I	V	G	C	W	M	J	L	S	H	B	I	P
B	S	D	W	T	V	H	X	K	V	J	V	J	Z	N

~~~~ *OBEDIENCE* ~~~~

Young people are taught to obey their parents, teachers, or other elders. Adults usually obey their spouse, supervisor, or follow certain rules of society. In many cases, disobedience can destroy families and relationships. However, our willingness to obey God and His commandments is the ultimate act of obedience. It also minimizes the trouble in our lives.

(Read & find the bold and underlined words)

8 Cause me to hear thy loving-kindness in the **morning**; for in thee
do I trust: cause me to know the way **wherein** I should walk; for I
lift up my soul unto thee. 9 **Deliver** me, O LORD, from mine
enemies: I flee unto thee to hide me. 10Teach me to do thy will; for
thou art my God: thy spirit is good; lead me into the land of
uprightness. *Psalm 143:8-10 (KJV)*

10 Since you have kept my command to endure **patiently**, I will
also keep you from the hour of **trial** that is going to come upon the
whole world to test those who live on the earth. 11 I am coming
soon. Hold on to what you have, so that no one will take your
crown. *Revelation 3:10-11 (NIV)*

1 Blessed are they whose ways are **blameless**, who walk according
to the law of the LORD. 2 Blessed are they who keep his statutes
and seek him with all their heart. 3 They do nothing wrong; they
walk in his ways. *Psalm 119:1-3 (NIV)*

If you will only **obey** the LORD your God, by **diligently** **observing**
all his commandments that I am **commanding** you today, the
LORD your God will set you high above all the nations of the earth;
2 all these blessings shall come upon you and **overtake** you, if you
obey the LORD your God… *Deuteronomy 28:1-2 (NRSV)*

OBEDIENCE

S	S	E	N	T	H	G	I	R	P	U	P	Z	B	W
E	Y	N	Y	Q	G	N	I	V	R	E	S	B	O	H
O	W	D	N	L	A	I	R	T	D	S	X	M	V	E
G	G	O	K	G	T	D	U	D	E	L	I	V	E	R
C	P	A	T	I	E	N	T	L	Y	O	D	A	R	E
N	Y	U	P	L	D	A	E	U	G	D	P	A	T	I
B	H	W	R	W	L	M	Q	G	N	H	V	H	A	N
E	P	D	G	X	A	M	W	T	I	O	K	R	K	W
J	F	S	O	L	H	O	K	C	N	L	H	S	E	O
T	M	L	B	X	X	C	W	I	R	H	I	K	O	R
V	B	R	E	P	W	S	S	R	O	Q	K	D	Q	C
R	P	P	Y	C	R	K	H	K	M	E	N	Z	D	N
A	H	N	S	A	F	C	L	W	P	Z	T	H	E	J
K	Z	S	C	R	C	B	W	N	E	Z	U	Z	B	X
Z	N	M	J	X	N	R	O	S	H	W	G	H	Z	L

~~~~ *PEACE* ~~~~

The presence of peace is the absence of disturbance or war. It takes great effort to keep peace – not only of the mind – but also in our relationships, home, school, church, and even our country. Jesus is known as the Prince of Peace. When He is in the midst…the problems dissipate.

(Read & find the bold and underlined words)

13 And **suddenly** there was with the angel a multitude of the **heavenly** host praising God, and saying, 14 Glory to God in the highest, and on earth peace, good will toward men. *Luke 2:13-14 (KJV)*

And he **arose**, and rebuked the wind, and said unto the sea, Peace, be still. And the wind **ceased**, and there was a great **calm**. *Mark 4:39 (KJV)*

Grace be unto you, and **peace**, from God our Father, and from the Lord Jesus Christ. *1 Corinthians 1:3 (KJV)*

A heart at peace gives life to the body, but **envy** rots the **bones**. *Proverbs 14:30 (NIV)*

Peace I leave with you; my peace I give you. I do not give to you as the world gives. Do not let your hearts be **troubled** and do not be **afraid**. *John 14:27 (NIV)*

Peacemakers who sow in peace raise a harvest of righteousness. *James 3:18 (NIV)*

Depart from evil and do good; Seek peace and pursue it. *Psalm 34:14 (NKJV)*

PEACE

P	E	A	C	E	M	A	K	E	R	S	T	R	U	C
H	E	A	V	E	N	L	Y	W	U	K	F	M	A	X
Q	T	R	O	U	B	L	E	D	C	V	F	T	K	O
T	O	O	W	O	P	A	D	I	J	B	K	T	G	Z
R	Y	S	N	D	D	E	S	A	E	C	P	S	G	Q
D	F	E	Y	V	N	E	R	R	T	J	A	X	R	W
N	S	I	Z	L	G	J	P	F	H	T	R	L	S	T
D	T	E	Y	T	W	F	I	A	V	T	M	R	M	A
L	X	Y	W	G	J	B	B	L	R	W	A	M	U	P
N	Q	W	Q	A	Z	Y	U	R	U	T	K	X	C	A
P	K	G	V	A	D	Q	Q	A	F	M	G	Q	S	B
R	R	N	C	P	C	F	J	K	J	I	W	Y	U	L
A	N	J	A	P	J	R	Y	X	J	P	F	V	A	F
Y	B	Q	W	C	Z	G	K	J	U	C	F	Y	F	I
Y	J	R	D	E	W	Q	D	E	D	Q	X	I	E	I

~~~~ *POWER* ~~~~

Power is displayed through energy, position, strength, personal influence, or divine authority. When power is abused, it destroys. When it is used properly, success follows. Believers in Christ serve a powerful – Almighty, God. Imitate Christ, and use power as a force for positive change.

(Read & find the bold and underlined words)

The voice of the LORD is **powerful**; the voice of the LORD is full of **majesty**. *Psalm 29:4 (KJV)*

Death and life are in the power of the tongue: and they that love it shall eat the fruit thereof. *Proverbs 18:21 (KJV)*

For the word of God is **alive** and powerful. It is sharper than the sharpest **two-edged** sword, cutting between soul and spirit, between joint and marrow. It exposes our **innermost** thoughts and desires. *Hebrews 4:12 (NLT)*

God has spoken once, Twice I have heard this: That power **belongs** to God. *Psalm 62:11 (NKJV)*

22 Out of the north comes golden **splendor**; around God is
awesome majesty. 23 The Almighty—we cannot find him; he is
great in power and **justice**, and abundant righteousness he will not
violate. *Job 37:22-23 (NRSV)*

3 He is the reflection of God's glory and the exact **imprint** of
God's very being, and he sustains all things by his powerful word.
When he had made **purification** for sins, he sat down at the right
hand of the Majesty on high, 4 having become as much **superior** to
angels as the name he has inherited is more excellent than theirs.
Hebrews 1:3-4 (NRSV)

POWER

N	I	G	E	Y	F	B	R	N	R	P	C	H	Q	R
B	O	F	C	H	U	B	E	E	T	A	L	O	I	V
S	Z	I	I	R	S	P	O	L	W	A	O	Z	U	O
X	F	I	T	H	M	Q	M	E	O	A	F	B	R	R
U	F	Q	S	A	S	F	S	V	E	N	S	K	Y	R
F	S	K	U	P	C	O	X	Z	D	S	G	P	T	G
I	O	I	J	A	M	I	R	A	G	Z	U	S	S	Z
Y	Q	W	M	E	L	U	F	R	E	W	O	P	E	W
J	X	A	B	P	D	I	E	I	D	M	Z	E	J	E
B	X	X	D	G	R	V	V	X	R	Y	U	N	A	S
N	W	J	I	R	O	I	R	E	P	U	S	D	M	B
C	G	D	O	L	R	Y	N	T	R	V	P	O	N	T
J	Y	K	J	L	D	N	V	T	G	C	U	R	L	Y
F	B	T	D	T	I	J	G	L	A	G	L	U	F	Y
L	Q	C	E	Z	Q	K	M	N	G	P	B	G	O	C

~~~~ *PRAISE* ~~~~

Children are praised for getting good grades, organizations are applauded for their contributions to society, and entertainers receive accolades for their humanitarian efforts. God is worthy of our praise because of His grace and mercy. Through Him, we are alive and He is the provider of all natural resources necessary to sustain life – for this, we exalt Him.

(Read & find the bold and underlined words)

Every day will I bless thee; and I will **praise** thy name for ever and ever. *Psalm 145:2 (KJV)*

1 I will praise you, O LORD, with all my heart; I will tell of all
your **wonders**. 2 I will be glad and **rejoice** in you; I will sing praise
to your name, O Most **High**. *Psalm 9:1-2 (NIV)*

To the end that my glory may **sing** praise to You and not be **silent**. O LORD my God, I will give **thanks** to You forever. *Psalm 30:12 (NKJV)*

Praise the LORD! Oh, give thanks to the LORD, for He is good! For His mercy endures forever. *Psalm 106:1 (NKJV)*

3 For I **proclaim** the name of the LORD: **Ascribe** greatness to our
God. 4 He is the Rock, His work is **perfect**; For all His ways are
justice, A God of truth and without injustice; Righteous and
upright is He. *Deuteronomy 32:3-4 (NKJV)*

Then a **voice** came from the **throne**, saying, "Praise our God, all you His servants and those who fear Him, both **small** and great!" *Revelation 19:5 (NKJV)*

PRAISE

P	R	O	C	L	A	I	M	J	H	C	Y	Y	R	A
H	T	N	E	L	I	S	P	T	G	T	K	E	J	J
F	K	D	L	N	S	R	C	D	H	N	J	R	R	I
G	E	A	E	F	A	E	B	R	V	O	I	C	E	A
B	M	G	S	I	F	D	O	N	I	W	R	S	I	N
S	K	G	S	R	A	N	P	C	T	B	Q	G	K	Q
X	I	E	E	K	E	O	E	J	B	Z	E	R	I	V
L	M	P	D	A	N	W	G	D	O	G	H	V	R	P
G	H	G	R	D	A	A	S	P	T	G	Z	L	C	C
P	P	S	I	Q	Z	F	H	J	M	E	R	D	V	Z
L	R	R	V	Q	S	B	G	T	Z	R	F	D	N	A
R	A	U	J	D	V	P	I	D	K	K	C	I	M	U
M	X	N	Q	A	T	R	H	W	T	V	X	I	W	Q
X	M	W	J	O	W	W	S	M	H	O	N	R	G	X
G	L	F	K	X	M	I	N	O	C	V	P	X	P	N

~~~~ *PRAY* ~~~~

God answers prayers. You can call upon Him – wherever you may be – to give thanks, ask for a blessing, or offer an intercessory prayer for someone else. He responds in His own time. We are to pray in Jesus' name, and we are advised to 'pray without ceasing' – this keeps us in touch with God.

(Read & find the bold and underlined words)

But thou, when thou **prayest**, enter into thy **closet**, and when thou hast shut thy **door**, pray to thy Father which is in secret; and thy Father which seeth in secret shall reward thee **openly**. *Matthew 6:6 (KJV)*

If my people, which are called by my name, shall humble themselves, and pray, and seek my face, and turn from their wicked ways; then will I hear from heaven, and will forgive their sin, and will heal their land. *2 Chronicles 7:14 (KJV)*

1 And it came to pass, that, as he was praying in a certain place,
when he ceased, one of his disciples said unto him, Lord, teach us
to pray, as **John** also taught his disciples. 2And he said unto them,
When ye pray, say, Our Father which art in heaven, **Hallowed** be
thy name. Thy kingdom come. Thy will be done, as in heaven, so
in earth. 3 Give us day by day our daily **bread**. 4And forgive us our
sins; for we also forgive every one that is indebted to us. And lead
us not into temptation; but **deliver** us from evil.
Luke 11:1-4 (KJV)

18 If I had **cherished** iniquity in my heart, the Lord would not have
listened. 19 But truly God has listened; he has given heed to the
words of my prayer. 20 Blessed be God, because he has not rejected
my prayer or removed his steadfast love from me.
Psalm 66:18-20 (NRSV)

PRAY

M	C	Q	I	Q	A	X	P	C	J	Y	D	B	H	V
L	D	R	O	O	D	N	H	O	J	X	O	X	H	W
I	I	E	C	T	S	E	Y	A	R	P	E	V	K	Q
S	I	M	L	K	R	N	W	V	A	N	O	A	B	V
T	I	U	O	I	D	K	Z	O	K	M	E	A	N	K
E	X	P	S	A	V	F	P	N	L	Y	V	D	M	S
N	A	H	E	M	T	E	W	Z	R	L	U	I	Y	W
E	E	R	T	M	N	I	R	T	E	E	A	W	H	Y
D	B	W	D	L	Q	N	V	N	C	B	L	H	D	P
W	A	V	Y	N	A	U	B	K	V	U	H	A	D	U
Y	J	E	O	R	E	H	T	I	M	C	I	V	O	R
P	V	P	Y	X	F	B	H	L	E	J	W	T	R	J
T	H	G	B	K	X	D	B	W	I	D	W	I	I	P
N	P	I	D	N	N	L	X	U	R	Q	D	K	R	H
S	E	W	V	T	L	M	L	P	K	O	S	N	Z	N

~~~~ *PRIORITIES* ~~~~

Our lives can be filled with so many desires and responsibilities – both negative and positive. If we don't take control and prioritize our life, we risk falling out of fellowship with God. When God is first in our life, everything else will move into its proper place.

(Read & find the bold and underlined words)

And thou **<u>shalt</u>** love the LORD thy God with all thine heart, and with all thy soul, and with all thy might. *Deuteronomy 6:5 (KJV)*

16 For everything in the world—the **<u>cravings</u>** of sinful man, the lust
of his eyes and the **<u>boasting</u>** of what he has and does—comes not
from the Father but from the world. 17 The world and its **<u>desires</u>**
pass away, but the man who does the will of God lives forever.
1 John 2:16-17 (NIV)

4 Don't wear yourself out trying to get rich. Be wise enough to
know when to quit. 5 In the **<u>blink</u>** of an eye wealth disappears, for
it will **<u>sprout</u>** wings and fly away like an **<u>eagle</u>**.
Proverbs 23:4-5 (NLT)

Let all things be done **<u>decently</u>** and in **<u>order</u>**.
1 Corinthians 14:40 (NKJV)

33 But strive first for the kingdom of God and his righteousness,
and all these things will be given to you as well. 34 "So do
not worry about **<u>tomorrow</u>**, for tomorrow will bring worries
of its own. Today's trouble is **<u>enough</u>** for today.
Matthew 6:33-34 (NRSV)

1 So if you have been **<u>raised</u>** with Christ, seek the things that are
above, where Christ is, seated at the right hand of God. 2 Set your
minds on things that are **<u>above</u>**, not on things that are on earth, 3
for you have died, and your life is hidden with Christ in God.
Colossians 3:1-3 (NRSV)

PRIORITIES

G	N	I	T	S	A	O	B	V	N	L	R	P	F	X
M	E	N	O	U	G	H	G	C	K	I	B	V	W	N
J	A	V	M	Z	O	N	C	H	D	H	J	U	D	Y
F	G	K	O	N	V	R	I	O	G	M	M	F	X	J
C	L	D	R	B	R	K	P	V	R	T	B	A	V	K
R	E	D	R	O	A	I	J	S	A	L	D	H	G	S
C	Y	U	O	I	T	D	E	S	I	R	E	S	M	C
T	M	O	W	I	A	M	H	N	S	A	C	P	T	D
M	A	F	T	P	I	F	K	X	E	V	E	A	M	U
J	D	F	U	C	X	T	L	J	D	T	N	E	W	Q
Q	U	I	Y	Z	D	W	T	E	A	G	T	C	U	A
F	I	Z	A	P	N	H	D	G	C	L	L	J	T	N
I	N	Q	R	M	T	L	U	X	A	D	Y	E	U	C
T	Y	S	V	W	N	F	M	H	V	O	Q	W	O	E
U	Z	F	O	K	C	L	S	G	C	L	B	G	Q	Z

~~~~ PROMISE ~~~~

Are you good at keeping promises? They are easy to make, yet sometimes hard to fulfill. People expect life partners to be faithful, politicians to keep their campaign promises, or everyday people to honor their word. God keeps His promises, and we are responsible for keeping our promises to Him.

(Read & find the bold and underlined words)

For I the LORD thy God will hold thy **<u>right</u>** hand, saying unto thee, Fear not; I will help thee. *Isaiah 41:13 (KJV)*

3 His divine power has given us everything we **<u>need</u>** for life and **<u>godliness</u>** through our knowledge of him who called us by his own glory and goodness. 4 Through these he has given us his very great and precious **<u>promises</u>**, so that through them you may **<u>participate</u>** in the divine nature and **<u>escape</u>** the **<u>corruption</u>** in the world caused by evil desires. *2 Peter 1:3-4 (NIV)*

Blessed is the man who endures **<u>temptation</u>**; for when he has been approved, he will receive the crown of life which the Lord has promised to those who love Him. *James 1:12 (NKJV)*

"Blessed be the LORD, who has given rest to His people Israel, according to all that He promised. There has not failed one word of all His good promise, which He promised through His servant **<u>Moses</u>**. *1 Kings 8:56 (NKJV)*

When the bow is in the **<u>clouds</u>**, I will see it and **<u>remember</u>** the everlasting **<u>covenant</u>** between God and every living creature of all flesh that is on the earth." *Genesis 9:16 (NRSV)*

PROMISE

J	H	A	X	C	W	C	R	V	T	E	A	P	W	F
T	S	P	R	O	M	I	S	E	S	D	U	O	L	C
C	S	T	I	V	E	L	M	C	B	E	D	X	O	L
J	E	I	G	E	K	P	A	Q	C	M	S	V	F	Y
B	N	A	H	N	T	P	J	K	I	L	E	O	G	C
G	I	W	T	A	E	A	M	B	B	Z	S	M	M	Y
R	L	X	T	N	N	E	P	L	G	U	A	V	E	F
Q	D	I	K	T	A	H	D	I	A	Z	U	C	O	R
N	O	I	T	P	U	R	R	O	C	S	L	L	R	K
N	G	E	L	F	Z	C	R	F	E	I	K	P	T	G
N	K	E	Z	P	Q	G	E	M	E	D	T	P	R	E
Y	B	D	T	K	R	Q	T	H	C	O	U	R	G	D
O	U	T	H	L	A	H	G	D	E	M	X	R	A	H
O	W	L	E	S	O	H	Q	F	U	H	L	F	W	P
T	M	M	F	I	T	A	O	O	W	T	C	B	I	U

~~~~ *PROSPERITY* ~~~~

An unknown author said, "In prosperity, our friends know us; in adversity, we know our friends." Financial wealth does not equate to spiritual wealth. To be prosperous is to be blessed by the Lord in many ways. Thanks to God for all that comes from Him.

(Read & find the bold and underlined words)

If they obey and serve him, they will spend the rest of their days in **prosperity** and their years in **contentment**. *Job 36:11 (NIV)*

The **blessing** of the Lord makes a person rich, and he adds no **sorrow** with it. *Proverbs 10:22 (NLT)*

People who **conceal** their sins will not prosper, but if they confess and turn from them, they will **receive** mercy. *Proverbs 28:13 (NLV)*

"And you shall remember the LORD your God, for it is He who gives you power to get wealth, that He may **establish** His covenant which He **swore** to your fathers, as it is this day. *Deuteronomy 8:18 (NKJV)*

This Book of the Law shall not depart from your mouth, but you shall **meditate** in it day and night, that you may observe to do according to all that is written in it. For then you will make your way **prosperous**, and then you will have good success. *Joshua 1:8 (NKJV)*

No weapon formed against you shall prosper, And every tongue which rises against you in judgment You shall condemn. This is the **heritage** of the servants of the LORD, And their righteousness is from Me," Says the LORD. *Isaiah 54:17 (NKJV)*

Beloved, I pray that you may prosper in all things and be in **health**, just as your soul prospers. *3 John 1:2 (NKJV)*

PROSPERITY

T	M	K	C	O	E	M	W	E	A	Y	N	R	D	O
N	U	R	O	T	B	X	O	V	T	S	U	T	W	H
E	M	M	H	X	N	Z	R	I	U	T	E	D	R	R
M	H	G	L	S	U	O	R	E	P	S	O	R	P	V
T	I	E	J	H	I	E	O	C	P	A	T	P	H	A
N	Q	Z	V	U	P	L	S	E	U	G	H	E	X	D
E	U	U	A	S	O	H	B	R	U	N	R	X	M	I
T	N	B	O	V	W	E	T	A	T	I	D	E	M	A
N	K	R	V	U	F	O	O	L	T	S	Q	J	X	R
O	P	F	E	J	K	J	R	A	A	S	G	X	W	H
C	V	A	H	W	H	L	G	E	Z	E	E	R	I	B
I	R	A	L	F	J	E	U	C	N	L	H	G	M	H
V	O	I	O	E	Z	A	B	N	W	B	O	K	K	O
M	U	C	H	Y	J	K	E	O	G	T	Z	J	P	N
G	H	K	N	T	J	D	J	C	H	T	K	U	D	Q

~~~~ REPENTANCE ~~~~

When you repent, you are preparing yourself for a new life in Christ Jesus. To be sorry internally, and not express your apology is useless. Sinners are expected to repent. Always seek God – for only He can turn your life around and bring healing.

(Read & find the bold and underlined words)

30 "Therefore, O house of Israel, I will judge you, each one
according to his ways, declares the **Sovereign** LORD. Repent!
Turn away from all your offenses; then sin will not be your
downfall. 31 Rid yourselves of all the **offenses** you have
committed, and get a new heart and a new spirit. Why will you die,
O house of Israel? 32 For I take no pleasure in the death of **anyone**,
declares the Sovereign LORD. Repent and live!
Ezekiel 18:30-32 (NIV)

In the same way, there is more joy in heaven over one lost sinner who repents and returns to God than over **ninety-nine** others who are righteous and haven't **strayed** away! *Luke 15:7 (NLT)*

14 If My people who are called by My name will humble
themselves, and pray and seek My face, and turn from their wicked
ways, then I will hear from heaven, and will forgive their sin and
heal their land. 15 Now My eyes will be open and My ears
attentive to prayer made in this place. 16 For now I have chosen
and sanctified this house, that My name may be there forever; and
My eyes and My heart will be there **perpetually**.
2 Chronicles 7:14-16 (NKJV)

19 Repent therefore and be **converted**, that your sins may be
blotted out, so that times of **refreshing** may come from the
presence of the Lord, 20 and that He may send Jesus Christ, who
was preached to you before … *Acts 3:19-20 (NKJV)*

REPENTANCE

P	S	S	T	R	A	Y	E	D	S	E	D	D	H	I
D	E	T	R	E	V	N	O	C	A	O	O	I	X	P
Q	D	R	C	F	V	E	Y	F	R	Y	M	Y	G	F
O	W	D	P	R	A	S	O	O	F	I	L	C	T	P
P	N	I	N	E	T	Y	N	I	N	E	W	E	P	B
D	H	T	N	S	T	P	L	D	H	E	N	E	K	W
J	G	M	I	H	E	U	L	S	Q	I	L	S	Z	F
X	I	A	T	I	N	S	A	X	B	S	V	T	E	J
Y	S	A	T	N	T	V	F	L	S	G	H	G	Y	S
T	S	W	D	G	I	S	N	S	L	H	Q	Y	Z	W
W	T	R	Q	P	V	D	W	N	Q	Y	V	N	J	J
N	G	I	E	R	E	V	O	S	T	W	U	Y	A	A
Y	Y	H	F	A	F	P	D	E	T	T	O	L	B	I
V	O	A	R	A	C	G	M	O	L	Y	I	R	D	D
R	C	B	P	I	P	V	J	K	Z	W	S	S	E	R

~~~~ RIGHTEOUSNESS ~~~~

Christians are expected to carry themselves in a morally upright manner. God has high standards and He expects the best from us so that we will become an example to others. It is through Jesus Christ that we become righteous for His namesake.

(Read & find the bold and underlined words)

7 But the LORD shall endure forever: he hath prepared his throne
for judgment. 8 And he shall judge the world in righteousness, he
shall **<u>minister</u>** judgment to the **<u>people</u>** in uprightness.
Psalm 9:7-8 (KJV)

For the eyes of the Lord are over the **<u>righteous</u>**, and his ears are open unto their prayers: but the face of the Lord is against them that do evil. *1 Peter 3:12 (KJ V)*

9 What shall we **<u>conclude</u>** then? Are we any better? Not at all! We
have already made the charge that **<u>Jews</u>** and **<u>Gentiles</u>** alike are all
under sin. 10 As it is written: "There is no one righteous, not even
one; 11 there is no one who understands, no one who seeks God.
Romans 3:9-11 (NIV)

Who is wise? Let him understand these things. Who is **<u>prudent</u>**? Let him know them. For the ways of the LORD are right; The righteous walk in them, But transgressors stumble in them. *Hosea 14:9 (NKJV)*

The hope of the righteous ends in **<u>gladness</u>**, but the **<u>expectation</u>** of the wicked comes to nothing. *Proverbs 10:28 (NRSV)*

17 But the wisdom that is from above is first pure, then **<u>peaceable</u>**,
gentle, and easy to be **<u>intreated</u>**, full of mercy and good fruits,
without partiality, and without **<u>hypocrisy</u>**. 18 And the fruit of
righteousness is sown in peace of them that make peace.
James 3:17-18 (KJV)

RIGHTEOUSNESS

Y	E	E	A	K	Y	E	X	R	F	B	D	W	O	R
D	A	L	A	Z	I	M	M	Y	O	F	G	I	I	I
S	L	B	J	H	L	N	F	I	T	E	C	G	Z	V
E	W	A	B	Y	F	O	T	N	R	Y	H	F	C	J
C	L	E	Q	P	M	A	E	R	S	T	Y	M	V	P
E	Y	C	J	O	T	D	E	M	E	G	G	L	E	D
U	C	A	B	C	U	T	H	O	L	A	J	K	G	D
E	U	E	E	R	S	R	U	A	I	C	T	A	A	F
R	B	P	P	I	F	S	D	I	T	V	K	E	F	Q
S	X	F	N	S	T	N	C	O	N	C	L	U	D	E
E	V	I	D	Y	E	L	P	O	E	P	O	E	V	I
J	M	Z	E	S	J	H	J	S	G	I	C	H	O	T
N	Y	K	S	B	D	W	X	K	V	T	O	M	W	J
V	N	K	G	N	Z	C	Y	I	T	J	K	J	K	D
E	S	H	E	Q	T	I	O	E	V	N	Q	B	P	Z

~~~~ *SALVATION* ~~~~

Salvation is a gift from God – it cannot be purchased because Jesus has already paid the price. He suffered by shedding His precious blood to save us from sin. It is only by the wonderful grace of God that we are saved!

(Read & find the bold and underlined words)

25 The LORD is good to those who wait for Him, To the soul who
seeks Him. 26 It is good that one should hope and wait **quietly** For
the salvation of the LORD. 27 It is good for a man to **bear** the yoke
in his **youth**. *Lamentations 3:25-27 (NKJV)*

Lead me in Your truth and teach me, For You are the God of my **salvation**; On You I wait all the day. *Psalm 25:5 (NKJV)*

10 He was in the world, and the world was made through Him, and
the world did not know Him. 11 He came to His own, and His own
did not receive Him. 12 But as many as received Him, to them He
gave the right to become children of God, to those who **believe** in
His name: 13 who were **born**, not of **blood**, nor of the will of the
flesh, nor of the will of man, but of God. *John 1:10-13 (NKJV)*

"Most assuredly, I say to you, he who hears My word and believes in Him who sent Me has everlasting life, and shall not come into judgment, but has **passed** from death into life. *John 5:24 (NKJV)*

8 But what does it say? "The word is **near** you, on your lips and in
your heart" (that is, the word of faith that we proclaim); 9 because
if you confess with your lips that Jesus is Lord and believe in your
heart that **God raised** him from the dead, you will be saved. 10 For
one believes with the heart and so is justified, and one confesses
with the mouth and so is saved. *Romans 10:8-10 (NRSV)*

SALVATION

S	R	B	U	W	O	G	O	D	P	S	K	D	I	A
R	A	E	N	B	Q	B	E	A	R	X	O	O	P	G
I	B	L	A	W	U	S	S	E	J	W	R	W	J	Y
Q	H	I	V	A	I	S	N	L	R	P	D	T	O	T
M	I	E	R	A	E	H	B	Q	R	C	J	V	A	B
E	N	V	R	D	T	I	L	N	W	R	B	V	N	U
T	V	E	D	X	L	I	O	M	B	O	S	R	C	P
Z	S	W	D	G	Y	X	O	X	R	B	T	Y	D	Z
K	M	W	F	Q	O	E	D	N	U	Q	K	M	U	U
O	B	F	F	C	U	Y	M	M	Y	S	D	D	M	V
R	U	H	L	O	T	W	J	L	A	X	V	Q	K	O
E	Z	D	B	H	H	E	I	M	U	R	W	A	W	A
U	M	D	W	G	G	Y	I	V	S	M	U	W	Y	B
H	F	Y	B	J	G	R	A	G	M	Y	M	O	B	E
X	B	F	F	K	S	R	R	F	R	Z	D	F	Q	R

~~~~ *SEEK* ~~~~

God knew you from the beginning, but do you know Him? There are so many religious beliefs and cult groups striving to gain attention so that they can build their own kingdom. Yet, none are greater than the Creator. Seek Christ Jesus – for He is the Lamb of God and we are the builders of His kingdom.

(Read & find the bold and underlined words)

And I say unto you, Ask, and it shall be given you; seek, and ye shall find; **knock**, and it shall be opened **unto** you. *Luke 11:9 (KJV)*

The LORD looks down from heaven on the sons of men to see if there are any who understand, any who **seek** God. *Psalm 14:2 (NIV)*

9 The LORD is a refuge for the oppressed, a **stronghold** in **times**
of trouble. 10 Those who know your name will trust in you, for you,
LORD, have never **forsaken** those who seek you.
Psalm 9:9-10 (NIV)

But seek first the kingdom of God and His righteousness, and all these things shall be **added** to you. *Matthew 6:33 (NKJV)*

O God, You are my God; Early will I seek You; My soul **thirsts** for You; My flesh longs for You… *Psalm 63:1 (NKJV)*

7 "Ask, and it will be given you; search, and you will find; knock,
and the door will be opened for you. 8 For everyone who asks
receives, and everyone who **searches** finds, and for everyone who
knocks, the door will be opened. *Matthew 7:7-8 (NRSV)*

10 **Glory** in his holy name; let the hearts of those who seek the
LORD rejoice. 11 Seek the LORD and his strength, seek his presence
continually. *1 Chronicles 16:10-11*

SEEK

C	X	L	C	E	Q	F	X	S	S	D	X	Q	K	H
D	O	Y	S	A	D	M	O	T	X	E	Z	B	H	M
R	K	N	H	E	D	Q	S	R	Y	D	M	Q	L	K
B	L	X	T	P	A	R	U	O	S	D	V	I	N	D
L	A	F	Y	I	I	R	F	N	B	A	B	P	T	Z
E	X	Q	K	H	N	Z	C	G	E	K	K	Y	A	O
M	V	O	T	U	O	U	L	H	N	E	J	E	H	C
W	H	S	M	K	N	O	A	O	E	E	X	V	N	R
Y	N	H	N	T	R	R	C	L	A	S	M	Z	R	S
C	W	A	O	Y	C	K	Z	D	L	O	T	L	Z	F
A	H	P	F	U	N	X	R	O	X	Y	G	Y	G	Z
X	M	Y	V	N	W	N	S	A	O	L	L	Q	O	A
D	N	Q	P	X	P	X	O	H	B	N	U	L	Q	A
O	F	W	X	T	H	A	M	H	U	B	C	H	T	W
F	L	O	Y	R	V	R	D	A	M	F	R	P	G	D

~~~~ SOUL ~~~~

The soul of mankind has been described as the life force or unique essence created by God. As a believer in Christ, evil forces will tempt you. Never compromise your soul for earthly things that negatively impact your life. When death overtakes our body, the soul will live on because it belongs to the Father.

(Read & find the bold and underlined words)

12 For he shall deliver the needy when he crieth; the poor also, and
him that hath no **helper**. 13 He shall spare the poor and needy, and
shall save the souls of the needy.14 He shall **redeem** their soul from
deceit and violence: and precious shall their blood be in his sight.
Psalm 72:12-14 (KJV)

Behold, all souls are **mine**; as the soul of the father, so also the soul of the son is mine: the soul that sinneth, it shall die. *Ezekiel 18:4 (KJV)*

35 For whoever wants to save his life will lose it, but whoever **loses**
his life for me and for the **gospel** will save it. 36 What good is it for
a man to gain the whole world, yet **forfeit** his soul?
Mark 8:35-36 (NIV)

...he **restores** my soul. He guides me in **paths** of righteousness for his name's sake. *Psalm 23:3 (NIV)*

26 And what do you **benefit** if you gain the whole world but lose
your own soul? Is anything worth more than your soul? 27 For the
Son of Man will come with his **angels** in the glory of his Father
and will judge all people according to their **deeds**.
Matthew 16:26-27 (NLT)

Come and hear, all you who fear God, And I will declare what He has done for my **soul**. *Psalm 66:16 (NKJV)*

SOUL

S	L	G	N	Q	B	M	S	I	F	H	F	M	D	Q
T	M	F	O	R	F	E	I	T	Y	I	C	R	V	A
H	E	L	P	E	R	E	R	N	V	G	Y	Q	H	F
O	E	U	C	O	U	D	K	H	E	L	R	R	V	J
S	R	O	T	L	D	E	E	D	S	E	S	O	L	N
R	L	S	R	I	V	R	M	C	K	L	C	V	E	O
M	E	D	Z	D	F	H	L	W	E	F	Z	W	Z	H
R	A	T	U	I	I	E	Y	G	T	I	A	J	L	C
G	G	M	A	H	P	H	N	N	V	N	T	M	Q	U
A	V	T	V	S	G	A	T	E	K	J	B	Z	T	P
X	O	F	O	N	Q	S	T	M	B	E	F	O	S	X
T	P	G	S	P	Y	F	J	H	S	N	E	M	M	C
P	L	U	U	O	R	X	S	Q	S	U	B	S	I	V
W	G	T	S	B	H	P	Q	T	L	N	D	D	D	Q
Z	E	W	C	N	M	H	Q	M	H	X	K	Z	Y	A

~~~~ *SPIRIT* ~~~~

Your spirit allows you to have a private relationship with God. There will be people or situations in life that try to steal your joy and drain your spirit. When this happens, seek God and take time for spiritual renewal so that you can hear the voice of the Lord manifest in your life. The characteristics of your spirit can be negative or positive; however, when you dwell in God's purpose a Christ-like spirit surrounds you – and people will know that you are a child of God.

(Read & find the bold and underlined words)

But the **fruit** of the Spirit is love, joy, peace, patience, **kindness**, goodness, faithfulness... *Galatians 5:22 (NIV)*

5 May the God who gives endurance and **encouragement** give you a spirit of **unity** among yourselves as you follow Christ Jesus, 6 so that with one heart and mouth you may glorify the God and **Father** of our Lord Jesus Christ. *Romans 15:5-6 (NIV)*

3 Do not let your adornment be merely **outward**—arranging the hair, wearing gold, or putting on fine **apparel**— 4 rather let it be the hidden person of the heart, with the **incorruptible** beauty of a gentle and **quiet** spirit, which is very precious in the sight of God. *1 Peter 3:3-4 (NKJV)*

The **human** **spirit** is the lamp of the LORD, searching every **inmost** part. *Proverbs 20:27 (NRSV)*

5 Jesus answered, "Most assuredly, I say to you, **unless** one is born of water and the Spirit, he cannot enter the kingdom of God. 6 That which is born of the flesh is flesh, and that which is born of the Spirit is spirit. *John 3:5-6 (NKJV)*

SPIRIT

T	M	P	V	O	R	O	N	F	U	V	U	M	T	E
I	N	V	V	L	C	L	A	P	P	A	R	E	L	A
U	H	E	D	X	G	T	S	O	M	N	I	B	F	W
R	M	B	M	E	H	K	W	G	U	U	I	S	O	J
F	D	C	I	E	F	N	I	M	Q	T	E	S	J	S
U	I	M	R	Y	G	B	M	W	P	J	W	W	L	C
G	F	D	T	X	A	A	S	U	Y	X	A	A	N	D
E	H	I	Z	I	W	W	R	I	H	F	P	O	R	M
A	N	Q	L	Q	R	R	C	U	V	W	B	O	L	D
U	D	B	W	F	O	I	M	U	O	G	C	O	N	O
W	Q	A	S	C	N	A	P	F	S	C	T	D	L	X
H	K	I	N	D	N	E	S	S	E	L	N	U	Y	E
V	A	I	P	V	B	Z	W	T	G	R	Q	E	C	R
S	V	I	O	B	F	C	W	K	C	R	K	X	Z	Q
M	X	Z	O	G	N	U	D	D	E	B	A	W	H	R

~~~~ *STRENGTH* ~~~~

Praying for God's strength will get you through many challenges. Sometimes, it is all you need to make it through the day. Mental and spiritual strength are just as important as physical strength. Continuously work on both areas, so that when the appropriate time comes, your light will shine both internally and externally. In the Book of Psalms, David tells us that God is our strength.

(Read & find the bold and underlined words)

The LORD is my light and my salvation; whom shall I fear? The LORD is the **strength** of my life; of whom shall I be afraid? *Psalm 27:1 (KJV)*

...but those who hope in the LORD will **renew** their strength. They will soar on wings like eagles; they will run and not grow **weary**, they will walk and not be faint. *Isaiah 40:31 (NIV)*

31 For who is God besides the LORD? And who is the Rock **except**
our God? 32 It is God who **arms** me with strength and makes my
way perfect. 33 He makes my feet like the feet of a deer; he **enables**
me to stand on the **heights**. 34 He **trains** my hands for battle; my
arms can bend a bow of **bronze**. *Psalm 18:31-34 (NIV)*

'And you shall love the LORD your God with all your heart, with all your soul, with all your mind, and with all your strength.' This is the first commandment. *Mark 12:30 (NKJV)*

You in Your mercy have led forth the people whom You have redeemed; You have guided them in Your strength to Your holy **habitation**. *Exodus 15:13 (NKJV)*

27 Honor and majesty are before him; strength and joy are in his
place. 28 Ascribe to the Lord, O **families** of the peoples, ascribe to
the Lord glory and strength. *1 Chronicles 16:27-28 (NRSV)*

STRENGTH

H	A	B	I	T	A	T	I	O	N	S	O	V	W	R
E	T	K	W	A	Y	Y	E	X	C	E	P	T	J	P
I	D	G	E	X	R	R	J	S	N	I	A	R	T	H
G	T	O	N	A	V	A	V	A	T	L	H	L	A	Y
H	R	W	E	E	A	B	B	E	R	I	G	L	S	Z
T	R	W	R	V	R	L	H	A	I	M	I	C	G	O
S	I	F	R	O	E	T	A	O	H	A	S	F	X	W
U	L	U	N	S	C	G	S	G	J	F	J	B	Y	L
P	B	Z	Q	L	A	Q	W	F	Y	K	Z	P	G	S
R	E	L	X	B	L	A	X	P	X	V	R	X	T	K
A	O	J	I	V	P	J	C	E	D	D	B	E	S	A
Q	U	K	E	N	P	X	U	G	H	F	Q	C	Z	W
X	Q	X	K	A	L	T	B	K	R	J	T	M	F	C
Z	V	K	I	J	S	S	D	K	K	G	O	C	P	H
L	U	J	F	P	H	C	Q	A	M	Q	G	S	G	E

~~~~ *SUCCESS* ~~~~

Reaching goals such as weight loss, attainment of wealth, record-breaking fundraising efforts, graduating from college, or climbing to the top of a mountain are considered stories of success. Failures can bring a person to a point where they cease efforts to cbtain success. Who do you depend upon for success? If you have not attained success – perhaps you have been climbing the wrong ladder. Although it is common to have a fear of failure, don't give up because God wants us to be successful. Give God the glory for His role in your success.

(Read & find the bold and underlined words)

In everything he did he had great **<u>success</u>**, because the LORD was with him. *1 Samuel 18:14 (NIV)*

O LORD, save us; O LORD, **<u>grant</u>** us success.
Psalm 118:25 (NIV)

Then I **<u>observed</u>** that most people are **<u>motivated</u>** to success because they envy their neighbors. But this, too, is **<u>meaningless</u>**—like **<u>chasing</u>** the wind. *Ecclesiastes 4:4 (NLT)*

Observe the requirements of the Lord your God, and follow all his ways. Keep the **<u>decrees</u>**, commands, **<u>regulations</u>**, and laws written in the Law of Moses so that you will be successful in all you do and **<u>wherever</u>** you go. *1 Kings 2:3 (NLT)*

2 Their purpose is to teach people wisdom and discipline, to help
them understand the **<u>insights</u>** of the wise. 3 Their **<u>purpose</u>** is to
teach people to live **<u>disciplined</u>** and successful lives, to help them
do what is right, just, and fair. *Proverbs 1:2-3 (NLT)*

SUCCESS

S	N	O	I	T	A	L	U	G	E	R	D	L	Y	L
S	K	P	N	N	S	I	N	G	O	E	E	P	L	Y
P	R	A	S	I	K	I	J	P	T	V	V	S	Q	J
T	R	B	I	C	S	W	U	A	Y	E	R	S	P	S
G	J	S	G	A	Q	R	V	I	N	R	E	E	H	X
L	G	U	H	I	P	I	F	H	T	E	S	L	E	Q
J	D	C	T	O	T	W	T	C	R	H	B	G	Q	O
F	H	C	S	O	Y	N	S	C	S	W	O	N	Z	X
P	X	E	M	X	L	Y	E	H	H	R	G	I	U	D
J	H	S	J	X	H	D	E	D	X	T	S	N	Y	W
D	I	S	C	I	P	L	I	N	E	D	C	A	S	N
Y	K	C	C	F	Y	Z	G	V	H	Q	W	E	W	X
L	S	H	T	P	N	E	J	Q	Q	Y	A	M	X	X
X	M	W	Q	S	Z	B	M	R	T	A	H	I	F	T
E	M	F	K	N	J	P	A	D	A	Q	S	Y	O	Y

~~~~ *TEACH* ~~~~

We can be taught the wrong things, but the power of teaching is the ability to correct what is wrong and allow knowledge and wisdom to prevail. The Bible reveals that teaching is a gift. It is a very noble profession. Every opportunity to elevate someone's mind is a contribution to the world.

(Read & find the bold and underlined words)

9 **<u>Instruct</u>** a wise man and he will be **<u>wiser</u>** still; teach a righteous man and he will add to his **<u>learning</u>**. 10 "The fear of the LORD is the beginning of wisdom, and knowledge of the Holy One is understanding. *Proverbs 9:9-10 (NIV)*

8 The Lord is good and does what is right; he shows the proper path to those who go **<u>astray</u>**. 9 He leads the humble in **<u>doing</u>** right, **<u>teaching</u>** them his way. *Psalm 25:8-9 (NLT)*

If your gift is **<u>serving</u>** others, serve them well. If you are a teacher, teach well. *Romans 12:7 (NLT)*

The teaching of your word gives light, so even the **<u>simple</u>** can understand. *Psalm 119:130 (NLT)*

These things we also speak, not in words which man's wisdom teaches but which the Holy Spirit teaches, **<u>comparing</u>** spiritual things with spiritual. *1 Corinthians 2:13 (NKJV)*

Those who are **<u>taught</u>** the word must **<u>share</u>** in all good things with their teacher. *Galatians 6:6 (NRSV)*

TEACH

C	L	E	I	U	U	N	Z	T	Z	E	H	B	Z	U
P	O	D	T	S	C	G	T	Z	D	L	L	D	Q	J
S	H	M	J	N	H	S	C	R	E	P	K	H	C	B
X	P	T	P	S	Y	A	U	A	P	M	S	T	D	S
J	E	M	Z	A	N	G	R	G	N	I	O	D	Z	M
Q	V	P	R	T	R	N	T	E	V	S	X	P	U	Y
H	T	T	T	M	I	I	S	U	V	B	I	G	E	I
W	S	H	K	N	N	H	N	U	L	V	W	J	Z	C
A	S	G	G	Z	I	C	I	G	N	I	V	R	E	S
C	C	V	N	U	F	A	Y	H	S	S	R	N	S	Q
F	X	P	V	J	A	E	P	E	S	F	N	V	H	I
Z	X	Z	J	D	L	T	R	L	C	W	R	R	C	T
R	V	J	H	N	O	H	F	K	S	X	T	U	N	G
G	Z	P	Y	T	K	V	D	X	U	N	R	A	F	I
J	U	Y	K	G	T	E	F	H	A	H	B	J	L	P

~~~~ *THANKFUL* ~~~~

We all have good and bad days, but every day of living are days of thanksgiving. We are thankful for the food we eat, but do we remember to give thanks for all other blessings. As givers and receivers, we should be thankful because we are beneficiaries of God's love.

(Read & find the bold and underlined words)

And he **<u>directed</u>** the people to sit down on the grass. Taking the five **<u>loaves</u>** and the two fish and looking up to heaven, he gave thanks and broke the loaves. Then he gave them to the disciples, and the disciples gave them to the people. *Matthew 14:19 (NIV)*

Let them offer **<u>sacrifices</u>** of thanksgiving and sing joyfully about his **<u>glorious</u>** acts. *Psalm 107:22 (NLT)*

And let the peace that comes from Christ **<u>rule</u>** in your hearts. For as members of one **<u>body</u>** you are called to live in peace. And always be thankful. *Colossians 3:15 (NLT)*

Be **<u>thankful</u>** in all **<u>circumstances</u>**, for this is God's will for you who belong to Christ Jesus. *1 Thessalonians 5:18 (NLT)*

15 Ever since I first heard of your strong faith in the Lord Jesus and
your love for God's people everywhere, 16 I have not **<u>stopped</u>**
thanking God for you. I pray for you **<u>constantly</u>**...
Ephesians 1:15-16 (NLT)

Enter into His **<u>gates</u>** with thanksgiving, And into His **<u>courts</u>** with praise. Be thankful to Him, and bless His name. *Psalm 100:4 (NKJV)*

THANKFUL

C	O	N	S	T	A	N	T	L	Y	Q	G	O	N	O
D	E	T	C	E	R	I	D	G	K	Y	F	A	B	A
R	U	L	O	A	C	E	R	S	L	C	R	H	T	N
V	O	B	U	R	C	I	L	U	R	M	W	U	L	H
E	Z	N	A	R	G	O	F	O	Z	M	I	U	A	H
E	U	O	V	H	A	K	U	I	A	Y	K	Z	N	P
U	Z	M	V	V	N	L	V	R	R	F	V	I	W	Q
E	P	A	E	A	L	G	T	O	T	C	T	M	S	A
N	F	S	H	M	U	P	P	L	D	S	A	Y	Q	D
Q	B	T	U	Y	M	Z	T	G	A	T	E	S	X	U
L	N	O	G	A	N	N	U	X	L	V	I	T	T	Y
S	X	P	D	H	B	M	Q	H	J	Y	U	A	P	O
G	S	P	I	Y	Y	O	L	R	A	Z	L	E	Y	M
O	S	E	C	N	A	T	S	M	U	C	R	I	C	Q
V	X	D	E	K	P	F	A	G	D	Q	B	W	Z	R

~~~~ *TRANSFORMATION* ~~~~

As human beings, many of us are blessed to grow from childhood to adulthood. In various parts of the world, seasons change from hot to cold. This is God's intended transformation of life and nature. To be a Christian is to be born again – becoming a new creature in Christ Jesus. This is the greatest transformation.

(Read & find the bold and underlined words)

And be not **<u>conformed</u>** to this world: but be ye transformed by the renewing of your mind, that ye may prove what is that good, and **<u>acceptable</u>**, and perfect, will of God. *Romans 12:2 (KJV)*

As the men watched, Jesus' **<u>appearance</u>** was transformed so that his face **<u>shone</u>** like the sun, and his **<u>clothes</u>** became as white as light. *Matthew 17:2 (NLT)*

It will **<u>happen</u>** in a moment, in the blink of an eye, when the last trumpet is blown. For when the trumpet sounds, those who have died will be raised to live forever. And we who are living will also be **<u>transformed</u>**. *1 Corinthians 15:52 (NLT)*

15 It doesn't matter whether we have been **<u>circumcised</u>** or not. What **<u>counts</u>** is whether we have been transformed into a new
creation. 16 May God's peace and mercy be upon all who live by
this **<u>principle</u>**; they are the new people of God. *Galatians 6:15-16 (NLT)*

10 And if Christ is in you, the body is **<u>dead</u>** because of sin, but the
Spirit is life because of righteousness. 11 But if the Spirit of Him
who raised Jesus from the dead dwells in you, He who raised Christ from the dead will also give life to your **<u>mortal</u>** bodies through His Spirit who dwells in you. *Romans 8:10-11 (NKJV)*

TRANSFORMATION

T	R	A	N	S	F	O	R	M	E	D	P	W	E	L
F	D	D	E	C	N	A	R	A	E	P	P	A	H	K
R	N	N	Z	O	O	A	V	S	W	Y	A	W	M	H
J	S	P	R	I	N	C	I	P	L	E	T	S	J	F
P	U	C	M	X	I	C	L	J	W	K	H	L	R	R
L	A	T	R	O	M	E	U	N	G	O	E	O	D	X
D	E	A	U	U	V	P	K	N	N	L	K	C	N	O
G	Z	F	C	L	O	T	H	E	S	T	J	Q	L	F
Q	C	R	N	Z	Z	A	S	Z	T	L	K	Z	J	Y
B	I	G	W	Z	P	B	Z	Q	N	Q	Y	V	O	R
C	F	I	B	P	I	L	J	U	U	Z	N	B	Y	P
A	G	D	E	A	D	E	M	R	O	F	N	O	C	H
S	O	N	X	J	K	F	I	R	C	J	U	E	J	N
U	O	W	I	S	Y	S	B	Q	K	S	U	E	D	G
U	B	D	T	Y	E	T	Z	D	Q	Y	K	Q	Z	S

~~~~ *TRUTH* ~~~~

Lies can hurt us, and the truth can sometimes be painful as well, but healing begins when we are honest. You don't have to be manipulative or run and hide. It is too stressful to spread lies and have that cloud over your head. Trust the Holy Spirit to comfort and protect you, and let the truth set you free.

(Read & find the bold and underlined words)

So God has given both his promise and his **<u>oath</u>**. These two things are **<u>unchangeable</u>** because it is impossible for God to lie. Therefore, we who have fled to him for refuge can have great **<u>confidence</u>** as we hold to the hope that lies before us. *Hebrews 6:18 (NLT)*

For the law was given by Moses, but grace and **<u>truth</u>** came by Jesus Christ. *John 1:17 (KJV)*

6 Listen, for I have worthy things to say; I open my lips to **<u>speak</u>**
what is right. 7 My mouth speaks what is true, for my lips detest
wickedness. *Proverbs 8:6-7 (NIV)*

If we claim to be without sin, we **<u>deceive</u>** **<u>ourselves</u>** and the truth is not in us. *1 John 1:8 (NIV)*

Surely you **<u>desire</u>** truth in the inner parts; you teach me wisdom in the inmost place. *Psalm 51:6 (NIV)*

All the paths of the LORD are mercy and truth, To such as keep His covenant and His **<u>testimonies</u>**. *Psalm 25:10 (NKJV)*

13 However, when He, the Spirit of truth, has come, He will guide
you into all truth; for He will not speak on His own **<u>authority</u>**, but
whatever He hears He will speak; and He will tell you things to
come. 14 He will glorify Me, for He will take of what is Mine and
<u>declare</u> it to you. *John 16:13-14 (NKJV)*

TRUTH

D	S	L	Y	X	B	I	U	Z	H	T	U	R	T	W
O	P	N	T	E	S	T	I	M	O	N	I	E	S	T
I	E	R	I	S	E	D	S	G	C	P	C	J	E	Q
G	A	X	R	J	I	G	P	H	D	N	F	W	Z	N
O	K	E	O	C	C	D	A	D	E	C	L	A	R	E
U	L	Q	H	P	D	N	U	D	G	V	B	B	J	T
R	H	B	T	Y	G	M	I	M	E	F	B	A	H	N
S	R	T	U	E	L	F	O	R	K	C	G	E	Z	I
E	N	Y	A	X	N	Q	L	G	D	B	E	B	F	W
L	C	B	C	O	X	L	A	T	B	L	N	I	F	V
V	L	W	C	A	H	U	U	C	L	T	X	V	V	Q
E	B	R	Q	Z	K	W	Z	G	M	K	Q	Q	K	E
S	S	G	X	G	Q	F	A	G	Y	I	M	A	E	U
I	M	W	T	P	Q	G	W	I	Q	I	Q	W	E	Z
Y	N	O	P	M	G	V	D	I	X	O	N	G	Y	A

~~~~ *UNDERSTANDING* ~~~~

When we communicate, we must ensure that listeners clearly comprehend our message. It is through learning and listening that we seek to understand and also to be understood. Because our finite minds are unlike the all-knowing God we serve, we must effectively use our logical power that is granted by God. Even before us, He knows the beginning and the end.

(Read & find the bold and underlined words)

5 Trust in the Lord with all your heart; do not **<u>depend</u>** on your own understanding. 6 Seek his will in all you do, and he will show you which path to take. *Proverbs 3:5-6 (NLT)*

And the peace of God, which passeth all understanding, shall keep your hearts and **<u>minds</u>** through Christ Jesus. *Philippians 4:7 (KJV)*

My mouth will speak words of wisdom; the **<u>utterance</u>** from my heart will give understanding. *Psalm 49:3 (NIV)*

<u>Discretion</u> will protect you, and understanding will **<u>guard</u>** you. *Proverbs 2:11 (NIV)*

I will **<u>pursue</u>** your commands, for you **<u>expand</u>** my understanding. *Psalm 119:32 (NLT)*

The wise are known for their understanding, and **<u>pleasant</u>** words are **<u>persuasive</u>**. *Proverbs 16:21 (NLT)*

The fear of the LORD is the beginning of wisdom, And the knowledge of the Holy One is **<u>understanding</u>**. *Proverbs 9:10 (NKJV)*

UNDERSTANDING

G	B	N	O	C	Y	S	P	E	H	D	Y	X	R	P
S	N	O	N	O	G	O	M	I	N	D	S	N	U	X
U	C	I	T	A	Q	G	E	Q	I	R	R	R	Y	Y
S	A	T	D	N	A	P	X	E	H	A	S	O	C	B
B	N	E	C	N	A	R	E	T	T	U	W	D	N	B
P	E	R	S	U	A	S	I	V	E	G	P	P	K	D
Y	G	C	R	T	Z	T	A	C	V	F	O	B	N	E
X	R	S	O	P	J	A	S	E	T	S	B	U	A	Z
A	C	I	A	I	Y	X	Q	R	L	Y	P	C	W	C
M	A	D	N	C	Q	T	D	D	E	P	E	N	D	S
C	E	O	P	W	B	U	K	I	P	D	I	Z	G	X
M	G	B	P	B	I	T	R	P	Q	D	N	P	T	T
Q	B	V	E	B	P	J	D	J	X	M	X	U	J	P
B	D	Z	Q	D	S	N	A	J	T	A	B	Z	F	S
Q	R	W	F	B	Q	V	L	N	L	L	L	F	Q	E

~~~~ *VICTORY* ~~~~

We live in world that thrives on competition – struggling to become the winner. Have you ever been told that "the battle is not yours, it's the Lord's?" We are victorious because we can depend on Him to be triumphant in all matters of life.

(Read & find the bold and underlined words)

3 He shall say: "Hear, O Israel, today you are going into battle
against your enemies. Do not be **<u>fainthearted</u>** or afraid; do not be
<u>terrified</u> or give way to **<u>panic</u>** before them. 4 For the LORD your
God is the one who goes with you to **<u>fight</u>** for you against your
enemies to give you victory." *Deuteronomy 20:3-4 (NIV)*

57 But thanks be to God! He gives us the victory through our Lord
Jesus Christ. 58 Therefore, my dear brothers, stand firm. Let
nothing move you. Always give yourselves fully to the work of the
Lord, because you know that your **<u>labor</u>** in the Lord is not in vain.
1 Corinthians 15:57-58 (NIV)

6 Now I know that the LORD saves His anointed; He will answer
him from His holy heaven With the saving strength of His right
hand. 7 Some trust in **<u>chariots</u>**, and some in horses; But we will
remember the name of the LORD our God. 8 They have bowed
down and fallen; But we have risen and **<u>stand</u>** upright. 9 Save,
LORD! May the King answer us when we call.
Psalm 20:6-9 (NKJV)

For whatever is born of God **<u>overcomes</u>** the world. And this is the **<u>victory</u>** that has overcome the world—our faith. *1 John 5:4 (NKJV)*

But thanks be to God, who in Christ always leads us in **<u>triumphal procession</u>**, and through us spreads in every place the **<u>fragrance</u>** that comes from knowing him. *2 Corinthians 2:14 (NRSV)*

VICTORY

D	V	I	Z	T	R	G	Y	H	G	N	T	O	N	J
V	E	A	S	R	U	X	Y	E	O	V	D	B	B	Y
I	Q	T	E	R	R	I	F	I	E	D	S	G	Z	A
C	H	A	R	I	O	T	S	R	L	P	B	C	E	W
T	M	D	N	A	T	S	B	D	Z	E	Y	Q	L	D
O	A	O	V	U	E	T	Q	Q	O	F	Z	J	O	R
R	B	V	S	C	C	H	S	M	M	E	A	J	J	O
Y	W	E	O	W	U	G	T	F	C	U	N	U	Y	A
L	H	R	G	N	W	L	J	N	T	O	W	C	P	G
Y	P	C	T	N	F	P	A	N	I	C	J	H	P	R
R	D	O	C	I	I	R	N	B	I	A	G	O	L	M
C	W	M	K	B	G	I	N	U	O	T	F	Q	P	W
P	J	E	L	A	H	P	M	U	I	R	T	Z	C	F
H	M	S	R	B	T	P	G	D	D	T	U	M	F	T
I	V	F	E	S	W	F	B	H	B	S	W	N	N	T

~~~~ *WISDOM* ~~~~

Maturity of knowledge, experience and judgment create wisdom. As long as we have the ability to learn and accept the teachings of Father God, who is the wisest of all, we will be fruitful. Solomon was a very wise man, but he was not perfect. It is wise to obey the Lord.

(Read & find the bold and underlined words)

Wisdom is the **principal** thing; therefore get **wisdom**: and with all thy getting get understanding. *Proverbs 4:7 (KJV)*

10 "The fear of the LORD is the beginning of wisdom, and
knowledge of the Holy One is understanding. 11 For through me
your days will be many, and years will be added to your life. 12 If
you are **wise**, your wisdom will reward you; if you are a **mocker**,
you alone will suffer." *Proverbs 9:10-12 (NIV)*

The fear of the LORD is the beginning of wisdom; all who follow his **precepts** have good understanding. To him belongs eternal praise. *Psalm 111:10 (NIV)*

Anyone, then, who **knows** the good he ought to do and doesn't do it, sins. *James 4:17 (NIV)*

Wisdom **rests** in the heart of him who has understanding, But what is in the heart of **fools** is made known. *Proverbs 14:33 (NKJV)*

Wisdom and knowledge will be the **stability** of your times, And the strength of salvation; The fear of the LORD is His **treasure**. *Isaiah 33:6 (NKJV)*

An **intelligent** mind **acquires** knowledge, and the ear of the wise seeks knowledge. *Proverbs 18:15 (NRSV)*

WISDOM

I	J	I	Y	A	V	A	D	L	Z	I	A	T	A	P
N	D	F	T	B	L	C	D	F	T	Q	E	W	X	U
T	F	M	I	O	B	Q	O	M	C	Y	U	K	P	Q
E	G	H	L	U	E	U	R	R	P	T	K	M	F	I
L	A	P	I	C	N	I	R	P	R	T	N	O	X	J
L	W	B	B	Y	W	R	R	E	K	C	O	M	G	D
I	A	Z	A	P	W	E	A	V	T	L	W	S	D	N
G	O	M	T	I	C	S	N	O	S	W	S	S	J	W
E	W	I	S	E	U	T	X	B	C	B	C	O	W	M
N	L	D	P	R	P	S	N	Z	L	W	X	X	B	U
T	O	T	E	L	L	L	U	N	Y	I	R	B	A	J
M	S	S	I	E	X	W	V	B	X	M	F	P	B	P
V	M	H	M	D	V	A	D	K	M	F	Y	A	I	U
H	W	C	D	J	T	B	P	E	D	N	G	G	B	Q
Q	A	O	D	V	R	Q	N	X	T	T	V	L	F	G

~~~~ *WORSHIP* ~~~~

Gathering at church is great time to share the love of Jesus Christ and worship Him in fellowship with other Christians. However, we are also expected to move beyond the walls of the church to serve as a witness and worship the Lord daily. The Bible commands that we pay homage to none other than Jesus Christ – giving Him all the glory and praise.

(Read & find the bold and underlined words)

Do not worship any other god, for the LORD, whose name is **<u>Jealous</u>**, is a jealous God. *Exodus 34:14 (NIV)*

9 You shall have no **<u>foreign</u>** god among you; you shall not bow
down to an **<u>alien</u>** god. 10 I am the LORD your God, who brought
you up out of **<u>Egypt</u>**. Open wide your **<u>mouth</u>** and I will fill it.
Psalm 81:9-10 (NIV)

Ascribe to the LORD the glory due his name; **<u>worship</u>** the LORD in the **<u>splendor</u>** of his holiness. *Psalm 29:2 (NIV)*

You must worship only the Lord your God. He is the one who will **<u>rescue</u>** you from all your **<u>enemies</u>**." *2 Kings 17:39 (NLT)*

23 But the hour is **<u>coming</u>**, and now is, when the true worshipers
will worship the Father in spirit and truth; for the Father is **<u>seeking</u>**
such to worship Him. 24 God is Spirit, and those who worship Him
must worship in spirit and truth." *John 4:23-24 (NKJV)*

4 All the earth worships you; they sing praises to you, sing praises
to your name.' 5 Come and see what God has done: he is **<u>awesome</u>**
in his deeds among mortals. *Psalm 66:4-5 (NRSV)*

WORSHIP

S	P	L	E	N	D	O	R	J	C	W	Z	D	J	M
M	S	E	I	M	E	N	E	N	G	F	S	V	W	I
D	C	E	M	G	O	A	L	M	O	U	T	H	Q	M
M	C	A	Y	S	L	S	U	R	N	P	H	Z	R	I
J	Q	P	I	O	P	I	E	S	J	W	L	C	L	E
C	T	I	U	H	B	I	X	W	A	E	G	Z	I	B
W	S	S	N	K	G	I	H	W	A	P	Q	D	C	R
K	D	Q	E	N	X	L	D	S	T	J	F	J	Q	N
N	B	W	I	E	U	C	S	E	R	H	S	A	V	I
Z	Y	M	L	X	K	F	T	T	I	O	E	M	N	O
D	O	C	A	E	W	I	F	I	R	H	W	D	X	Z
C	J	I	Q	V	J	Y	N	L	U	L	W	R	S	K
O	Z	B	A	Y	D	P	P	G	I	P	H	Y	R	N
R	G	H	A	S	X	Y	Q	U	J	T	V	G	D	Q
Z	Q	D	F	F	P	I	V	P	Z	T	W	J	W	M

~~~~ *ZEAL* ~~~~

Christians who express great enthusiasm for the Lord and devote majority of their time to various ministries are often described as religious fanatics. If Jesus, who shed his blood for the remission of sin, has blessed you and your family, and you abide in His Word – how can you *not* have zeal for such an Awesome God?

(Read & find the bold and underlined words)

It is not good to have zeal without knowledge, nor to be **<u>hasty</u>** and miss the way. *Proverbs 19:2 (NIV)*

Never be **<u>lacking</u>** in zeal, but keep your spiritual **<u>fervor</u>**, serving the Lord. *Romans 12:11 (NIV)*

As many as I love, I **<u>rebuke</u>** and **<u>chasten</u>**. Therefore be zealous and repent. *Revelation 3:19 (NKJV)*

But it is good to be **<u>zealous</u>** in a good thing always, and not only when I am **<u>present</u>** with you. *Galatians 4:18 (NJKV)*

Even so you, since you are zealous for **<u>spiritual</u>** gifts, let it be for the edification of the **<u>church</u>** that you seek to **<u>excel</u>**. *1 Corinthians 14:12 (NKJV)*

ZEAL

E	R	L	U	S	E	U	Z	S	R	G	Z	U	W	M
R	J	K	C	G	J	T	P	T	H	E	N	V	K	F
P	P	D	H	G	N	I	K	C	A	L	B	B	K	N
B	X	D	A	E	R	J	R	L	S	P	K	U	T	V
J	U	Z	S	I	N	U	O	H	T	U	K	K	K	A
C	M	E	T	G	H	U	V	K	Y	T	V	L	H	E
N	R	U	E	C	S	C	R	D	X	S	S	O	X	S
P	A	S	N	X	F	Y	E	W	V	X	V	I	P	V
L	Y	L	Z	G	C	W	F	J	P	I	I	W	Z	J
B	Q	L	O	Q	V	E	P	D	E	S	A	F	F	C
S	Y	D	K	V	T	T	L	A	M	N	V	T	G	P
A	F	N	C	M	N	E	R	I	Q	E	O	V	V	P
C	O	Q	X	M	J	Y	C	L	V	A	S	W	U	X
Q	Y	K	M	L	R	I	U	F	M	S	K	O	H	F
V	U	M	I	W	N	R	M	N	E	J	X	C	O	M

~~~~ *KNOWING GOD* ~~~~

God – the Creator – is Omnipresent, Jesus is the Messiah, and the Holy Spirit is our Comforter. God loves unwaveringly and He is forgiving. The way to eternal life is through Jesus. He is waiting for all to accept Him as their personal Savior and to spread the Good News. We are to boldly proclaim His holy name.

(Read & find the bold and underlined words)

1 In the beginning God **created** the heaven and the earth. 2 And the
earth was without form, and void; and darkness was upon the face
of the deep. And the Spirit of God moved upon the face of the
waters. 3 And God said, Let there be light: and there was light.
Genesis 1:1-3 (KJV)

Behold, a **virgin** shall be with child, and shall bring forth a son, and they shall call his name **Emmanuel**, which being **interpreted** is, God with us. *Matthew 1:23 (KJV)*

And Jesus said unto them, I am the bread of life: he that cometh to me shall never **hunger**; and he that **believeth** on me shall never thirst. *John 6:35 (KJV)*

9 That if you confess with your mouth, "**Jesus** is Lord," and believe
in your heart that God raised him from the dead, you will be saved.
10 For it is with your heart that you believe and are justified, and it
is with your mouth that you confess and are saved.
Romans 10:9-10 (NIV)

And **suddenly** a voice came from heaven, saying, "This is My beloved Son, in whom I am well **pleased**." *Matthew 3:17 (NKJV)*

But Jesus looked at them and said to them, "With men this is impossible, but with God all things are **possible**." *Matthew 19:26 (NKJV)*

KNOWING GOD

I	P	O	S	S	I	B	L	E	H	J	H	K	V	I
N	P	Y	H	C	R	E	A	T	E	D	R	A	H	V
T	F	Y	L	X	U	D	E	S	A	E	L	P	T	M
E	Z	W	A	N	K	V	U	V	R	N	F	I	B	P
R	R	M	A	V	E	S	S	G	W	B	I	R	O	X
P	O	M	O	I	H	D	E	Y	I	F	B	C	D	G
R	M	T	L	R	L	S	D	Y	H	U	P	P	U	B
E	W	E	D	G	O	W	P	U	Y	M	E	N	T	I
T	B	O	A	I	K	W	N	W	S	H	J	D	H	H
E	J	E	T	N	Q	G	P	U	R	U	L	R	V	L
D	V	W	A	T	E	R	S	A	V	L	K	N	F	H
G	L	X	D	R	H	C	D	L	Q	R	C	A	R	E
K	V	O	E	Y	T	D	E	N	J	V	W	W	V	W
U	Y	Q	G	B	J	H	P	X	M	I	B	R	B	F
F	R	V	K	L	J	S	Q	N	T	R	J	T	W	P

~~~~ *CHILD OF GOD* ~~~~

There are many neglected children around the world who need attention. Children are a blessing and they are precious to God. A commitment to be responsible for them, love, nurture, and provide for them is what God expects from parents and guardians. When children come to know God, they will honor Him and continue the building of his Kingdom. Even as an adult, you are a child of the King. He protects His own.

(Read & find the bold and underlined words)

In the fear of the LORD there is strong **confidence**, And His children will have a place of refuge. *Proverbs 14:26 (NKJV)*

2 Beloved, now we are **children** of God; and it has not yet been
revealed what we shall be, but we know that when He is revealed,
we shall be like Him, for we shall see Him as He is. 3 And
everyone who has this hope in Him purifies himself, just as He is
pure. 4 Whoever commits sin also commits lawlessness, and sin is
lawlessness. *1 John 3:2-4 (NKJV)*

But Jesus said, "Let the little children come to Me, and do not **forbid** them; for of such is the kingdom of heaven." *Matthew 19:14 (NKJV)*

Behold, children are a **heritage** from the LORD, The fruit of the **womb** is a **reward**. *Psalm 127:3 (NKJV)*

Grandchildren are the crown of the aged, and the glory of children is their parents. *Proverbs 17:6 (NRSV)*

Train children in the right way, and when old, they will not **stray**. *Proverbs 22:6 (NRSV)*

CHILD OF GOD

N	H	M	D	Q	Y	D	B	D	S	S	E	E	M	B
Q	E	W	Y	L	F	M	N	Y	X	H	T	E	L	D
P	E	R	D	A	O	Q	Y	R	F	J	S	T	M	Q
X	K	C	D	W	R	Y	Y	E	D	E	G	Y	L	V
P	D	G	N	L	B	T	O	W	G	C	A	B	W	T
Q	J	N	P	E	I	I	S	A	C	H	K	O	A	I
C	N	H	R	S	D	H	T	R	A	I	N	B	K	B
H	E	O	B	S	B	I	C	D	J	I	Z	H	W	N
Z	W	C	W	N	R	G	F	D	S	W	M	E	W	D
Q	X	U	E	E	H	A	S	N	N	U	D	G	V	F
R	S	L	H	S	X	Q	K	M	O	A	P	T	Y	Q
E	T	C	N	S	L	Y	U	O	L	C	R	B	J	Q
G	Z	H	C	F	F	S	W	J	H	S	H	G	A	D
N	D	X	X	B	B	X	U	P	G	K	J	O	G	F
A	S	X	V	D	F	A	B	A	C	N	K	G	L	Q

~~~~ *THE TWELVE DISCIPLES* ~~~~

The Disciples were the original group of men who Jesus taught and entrusted to spread the gospel. After full authority by Christ, they became Apostles. Believers in Christ are also disciples of Jesus Christ. We are to study His Word, obey the Word, and spread the gospel. We are a part of God's divine plan.

(Read & find the bold and underlined words)

1 And when he had called unto him his twelve disciples, he gave
them power against unclean spirits, to cast them out, and to heal all
manner of sickness and all manner of disease. 2 Now the names of
the twelve apostles are these; The first, **Simon**, who is called Peter,
and **Andrew** his brother; **James** the son of Zebedee, and **John** his
brother; 3 **Philip**, and **Bartholomew**; **Thomas**, and **Matthew** the
publican; James the son of Alphaeus, and Lebbaeus, whose
surname was **Thaddaeus**; 4 Simon the **Canaanite**, and **Judas**
Iscariot, who also betrayed him. *Matthew 10:1-4 (KJV)*

17 Now Jesus, going up to Jerusalem, took the twelve **disciples**
aside on the road and said to them, 18 "Behold, we are going up to
Jerusalem, and the Son of Man will be betrayed to the chief
priests and to the scribes; and they will condemn Him to death, 19
and deliver Him to the Gentiles to mock and to scourge and to
crucify. And the third day He will rise again."
Matthew 20:17-19 (NKJV)

And he **ordained** twelve, that they should be with him, and that he might send them forth to **preach**... *Mark 3:14 (KJV)*

THE TWELVE DISCIPLES

C	P	N	O	M	I	S	Q	U	N	R	B	Q	Z	I
Q	A	I	I	X	E	R	R	Z	L	M	A	U	Z	Y
Z	P	N	L	M	O	S	X	J	S	O	R	T	B	H
C	Y	T	A	I	E	E	P	U	R	N	T	X	I	C
I	T	J	Y	A	H	L	D	D	E	Q	H	C	L	S
V	D	L	O	C	N	P	A	A	Z	Q	O	U	D	X
U	J	E	W	H	F	I	F	S	B	S	L	U	G	Z
R	X	X	W	W	N	C	T	D	U	P	O	I	T	C
F	B	Q	L	E	S	S	Q	E	Y	R	M	D	H	Q
R	S	M	D	H	R	I	A	T	R	E	E	N	O	Z
U	X	A	N	T	D	D	G	M	A	A	W	J	H	K
Y	T	A	S	T	D	B	N	G	O	C	I	R	E	O
D	W	I	Z	A	H	D	M	A	X	H	B	O	U	I
Q	B	K	H	M	L	S	G	Z	J	M	T	Y	Y	I
Y	L	T	O	N	Z	E	O	Y	J	V	K	I	L	R

~~~ *WOMEN IN THE BIBLE* ~~~

The Bible reveals the life and experiences of women. It shares their stories of strength, tragedy, faith, love, and obedience to God. Some are more prominent than others, yet their stories are equally important. Every message serves as guidance for our lives. The characteristics of a "virtuous woman" are described in Proverbs 31. When we seek to understand each woman's story, we will discover how significant women are in the Bible.

(Read & find the bold and underlined words)

8 So the women **hurried** away from the tomb, afraid yet filled with
joy, and ran to tell his disciples. 9 Suddenly Jesus met them.
"Greetings," he said. They came to him, **clasped** his feet and
worshiped him. *Matthew 28:8-9 (NIV)*

****

Eve was the first woman to experience the **miracle** of childbirth. Her life begins in Genesis. God created Eve to become Adam's **companion**.

Mary, the wife of Joseph, was the **mother** of Jesus.

Elisabeth, a righteous woman, was the mother of John the Baptist.

Deborah – the prophetess and judge – was known as a great military **commander**.

Rebekah was the wife of Isaac and the mother of twin boys - Esau and Jacob.

Ruth, an obedient Moab woman and an ancestor of Jesus, was committed to helping Naomi, her mother-in-law.

Mary **Magdalene** witnessed the **crucifixion** and the **resurrection** of Jesus Christ.

WOMEN IN THE BIBLE

O	V	U	O	M	A	G	D	A	L	E	N	E	C	B
M	I	P	I	H	Q	K	C	B	T	O	J	V	O	P
E	R	J	X	R	H	U	R	R	I	E	D	Q	N	S
T	F	K	R	D	E	H	U	T	J	Q	V	D	C	D
P	D	E	P	S	A	L	C	X	T	D	C	E	R	Z
I	A	Y	I	K	P	E	I	N	Y	R	L	I	H	M
L	N	Q	E	E	R	O	F	S	M	C	B	G	W	W
S	B	B	D	R	N	O	I	N	A	P	M	O	C	A
M	E	X	U	B	M	X	X	R	N	B	D	R	D	F
R	C	S	W	E	E	F	I	R	M	T	E	U	H	F
R	E	D	N	A	M	M	O	C	K	U	B	T	P	T
R	V	H	X	P	X	L	N	F	J	H	O	H	H	B
Y	T	P	T	H	M	B	A	O	P	T	R	X	T	E
L	G	K	P	O	J	T	M	O	Y	A	A	E	C	B
H	H	Y	K	J	M	R	L	X	O	W	H	B	Z	P

~~~~ *THE BEATITUDES* ~~~~

Jesus taught the Disciples from the mountain. *The Beatitudes* describe what is in store for those who are blessed and bound for eternal life. Recorded in the Gospel of Matthew, Jesus' message was delivered in the *Sermon on the Mount.*

(Read & find the bold and underlined words)

3 **Blessed** are the poor in spirit: for theirs is the kingdom of heaven.

4 Blessed are they that **mourn**: for they shall be comforted.

5 Blessed are the meek: for they shall **inherit** the earth.

6 Blessed are they which do **hunger** and **thirst** after righteousness: for they shall be filled.

7 Blessed are the **merciful**: for they shall obtain mercy.

8 Blessed are the pure in heart: for they shall see God.

9 Blessed are the **peacemakers**: for they shall be called the children of God.

10 Blessed are they which are **persecuted** for righteousness' sake: for theirs is the kingdom of heaven.

11 Blessed are ye, when men shall **revile** you, and persecute you, and shall say all **manner** of evil against you falsely, for my sake.

12 Rejoice, and be exceeding glad: for great is your **reward** in **heaven**: for so persecuted they the prophets which were before you. *Matthew 5:3-12* (KJV)

THE BEATITUDES

Z	D	E	T	U	C	E	S	R	E	P	N	W	P	B
B	R	N	L	G	N	Y	U	D	E	O	Y	X	X	E
C	W	L	N	I	I	B	Y	A	I	G	M	Q	O	H
T	K	U	T	X	V	L	C	Q	B	A	N	B	L	H
Q	P	F	S	A	H	E	I	K	D	U	X	U	G	V
S	I	I	J	L	M	S	R	Q	D	P	L	S	H	Y
W	N	C	T	A	O	S	Y	N	E	Y	T	O	O	U
D	H	R	K	I	U	E	X	L	P	Z	A	U	S	X
D	E	E	L	B	R	D	E	Z	T	U	K	Y	H	M
R	R	M	A	N	N	E	R	S	E	F	F	Z	P	Y
S	I	L	Z	V	C	E	Z	A	W	U	G	A	E	W
F	T	C	M	P	E	V	L	S	W	N	K	X	C	L
F	O	W	M	U	J	N	M	M	Q	E	G	U	D	M
G	F	W	D	N	A	R	L	T	H	I	R	S	T	Z
S	T	T	A	B	U	L	D	H	C	L	M	L	R	I

MY SPIRITUAL COMPANION

"Thy word is a lamp unto my feet, and a light unto my path."
Psalm 119:105 (KJV)

My favorite words:

My favorite Scriptures:

My promise for spiritual growth:

Date ______________________________

~~~~~~ *ACKNOWLEDGMENTS* ~~~~~~

for Prayers, Support, and Encouragement
beyond measure

Morton Branham
Chris Allen
Brenda Hogan

Carol Allen
Ceasar Gaiters
Cedric and Tasha Parks
Charlene Castonguay
Cormartie and Pam Zachery
Dawn Cooper
Derric Crowther, Esq.
Donny Allen
Dorothy Foster
Dr. Patricia Payne
Dr. Thomas D. Johnson, Sr.
and Mrs. Donna Johnson
Faye Johnson
George and Florence Blake
Hope Hillsman
Inez Allen
James "Jimmy" Allen
John and Vickie Harden
John Haysbert
Karen Johnson
Larry Cannon
LaWanda Johnson
Linda Hawkins
Made Men MC
Marcella Byrd
Mark Brown
Martin Harris
Mayor Rhine McLin, City of Dayton
Melvin Sharpe, Esq.
Mike and Loretta Combs
Mt. Enon Missionary Baptist Church
Nelson and Loree Reid
Otis Branham
Pamela Sotherland-Clark
Phyllis Jeffers-Coly
Rev. Dana and Mrs. Shalonda Owens
Rev. Dr. Harold Cottom, III
Rev. Dr. Robert E. Baines, Jr.
and Mrs. Daphene Baines
Rhonda Bogan
Richard and Verita Robinson
Ricky and Katrina Allen
Ruth McCorry
Shirley Byrd
Tara McCormick
Trinity Presbyterian Church
Vanessa Thomas
Willis and Regina Blackshear

Soul of the Pen Authors:
Marcella Ashe
Valerie Coleman
Dr. Kaye Manson Jeter
Gail Miller
Dorinda Nusum

About the Author

LaTonya Branham was born and raised in Ohio. She is also the author of CultureSeek. LaTonya earned a Master of Arts degree from Antioch University McGregor and a Bachelor of Science degree from Wilberforce University. She is a founding member of the Soul of the Pen Literary Group. Currently, she serves as the Associate University Registrar and as an adjunct professor at Central State University in Wilberforce, Ohio. LaTonya and her husband, Morton, currently serve in community outreach and youth ministries at the Mt. Enon Missionary Baptist Church in Dayton, Ohio.

For more information, please visit her web site:
www.LaTonyaBranham.com

Books by LaTonya Branham

ORDER FORM

We hope that you find books by LaTonya Branham to be interesting, engaging, and of great value. Please share this order form with your family and friends.

Send order form and payment to:
BabyStar Productions
P.O. Box 1271
Dayton, OH 45401-1271

****

Yes, I would like to place an order. I have indicated below which books I am ordering. I have enclosed a check or money order payable to ***Babystar Productions***, to cover my purchase.

Title	Item #	Price	Qty	Total
Spirit Seek	LB2	12.95	___	______
CultureSeek	LB1	8.00	___	______
		Subtotal		______
(Add $3.00 per book)		Shipping & Handling		______
		Total Enclosed		______

Your Information:
Name ____
Mailing address ______________________________
City, State, Zip ______________________________
E-mail address _______________________________

Please visit our website: www.LaTonyaBranham.com
THANK YOU!